Quantitative Methods

Economics Express

PEARSON

At Pearson, we take learning personally. Our courses and resources are available as books, online and via multi-lingual packages, helping people learn whatever, wherever and however they choose.

We work with leading authors to develop the strongest learning experiences, bringing cutting-edge thinking and best learning practice to a global market. We craft our print and digital resources to do more to help learners not only understand their content, but to see it in action and apply what they learn, whether studying or at work.

Pearson is the world's leading learning company. Our portfolio includes Penguin, Dorling Kindersley, the Financial Times and our educational business, Pearson International. We are also a leading provider of electronic learning programmes and of test development, processing and scoring services to educational institutions, corporations and professional bodies around the world.

Every day our work helps learning flourish, and wherever learning flourishes, so do people.

To learn more please visit us at: **www.pearson.com/uk**

Quantitative Methods

Ian Jacques

PEARSON

Harlow, England • London • New York • Boston • San Francisco • Toronto • Sydney
Auckland • Singapore • Hong Kong • Tokyo • Seoul • Taipei • New Delhi
Cape Town • São Paulo • Mexico City • Madrid • Amsterdam • Munich • Paris • Milan

Economics Express

PEARSON EDUCATION LIMITED
Edinburgh Gate
Harlow CM20 2JE
United Kingdom
Tel: +44 (0)1279 623623
Web: www.pearson.com/uk

First published 2013 (print)

The Financial Times. With a worldwide network of highly respected journalists, *The Financial Times* provides global business news, insightful opinion and expert analysis of business, finance and politics. With over 500 journalists reporting from 50 countries worldwide, our in-depth coverage of international news is objectively reported and analysed from an independent, global perspective. To find out more, visit www.ft.com/pearsonoffer.

ISBN: 978-0-273-77616-1 (print)
       978-0-273-77618-5 (PDF)
       978-0-273-78557-6 (eText)

British Library Cataloguing-in-Publication Data
A catalogue record for the print edition is available from the British Library

Library of Congress Cataloging-in-Publication Data
A catalogue record for the print edition is available from the Library of Congress
Jacques, Ian, 1957–
  Economics express: quantitative methods/Ian Jacques.
     pages cm
  Includes index.
  ISBN 978-0-273-77616-1
  1. Economics–Mathematical models.   2. Economics, Mathematical.   I. Title.
  HG135.J318 2013
  330.01'519–dc23
                                    2013019287

10 9 8 7 6 5 4 3 2 1
17 16 15 14 13

Print edition typeset in 9.5/12.5 pt Scene std by 71
Print edition printed and bound in Great Britain by Henry Ling Ltd., at the Dorset Press, Dorchester, Dorset

Contents

Supporting Resources

→ **Understand key concepts quickly**

Printable versions of the **Topic maps** give an overview of the subject and help you plan your revision

Test yourself on key definitions with the online **Flashcards**

→ **Revise effectively**

Check your understanding and practise for exams with the **multiple choice questions**

→ **Improve your confidence**

Attempt the **Specimen Examination Questions** and compare your answers with the worked solutions provided.

All this and more can be found at www.pearsoned.co.uk/econexpress

Introduction – Economics Express series

From the series editor, Professor Stuart Wall

Welcome to *Economics Express* – a series of short books to help you to

- take exams with confidence
- prepare for assessments with ease
- understand quickly
- and revise effectively

There has never been a more exciting time to study economics, given the shock to so many individuals, institutions and countries in 2007/8 when long established economic certainties were suddenly brought into question. The so-called 'credit crunch' overpowered both financial and non-financial organisations. Government bail-outs of banks and businesses became the order of the day in many countries, with massive increases in government expenditures to fund these bail-outs, quickly followed by austerity budgets aimed at restoring national debts and budget deficits to pre-credit crunch levels. Looking forward, there is as much talk about 'triple-dip' recessions as there is about recovery.

As you embark on your economic journey, this series of books will be your companions. They are not intended to be a replacement for the lectures, textbooks, seminars or further reading suggested by your lecturers. Rather, as you come to an exam or an assessment, they will help you to revise and prepare effectively. Whatever form your assessment takes, each book in the series will help you build up the skills and knowledge to maximise your performance.

> You can find more detail of the features contained in this book and which will help develop your assessment skills in the 'Guided Tour' on page ix.

Acknowledgements

I would like to thank my wife, Victoria, for her careful checking of the manuscript, and her suggestions on how the text could be improved.

Ian Jacques

Series editor's acknowledgements

I am extremely grateful to Kate Brewin and Gemma Doel at Pearson Education for their key roles in shaping this series. I would also like to thank the many lecturers and students who have so helpfully reviewed the key features of this series and whose responses have encouraged us to believe that many others will also benefit from the approaches we have adopted throughout this series.

Stuart Wall

Guided tour

→ ## Understand key concepts quickly

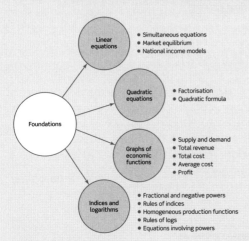

Start to plan your revision using the **Topic maps**.

Grasp **Key definitions** quickly using this handy box. Use the flashcards online to test yourself.

Key definition

The 95% confidence interval for a population mean is the range from

$$\bar{x} - 1.96\frac{\sigma}{\sqrt{n}} \text{ to } \bar{x} + 1.96\frac{\sigma}{\sqrt{n}}.$$

→ ## Revise Effectively

Assessment question

Could you answer this question? Guidelines on answering the question are presented at the end of this chapter.

A firm's fixed costs are 66 and the variable costs are 2 per unit. The corresponding profit function is $\pi = aQ^2 + bQ + c$.

(a) Write down expressions for the total and average cost functions, and sketch their graphs.

(b) Explain why $c = -66$.

(c) The firm makes a loss of 18 when $Q = 2$ and a profit of 24 when $Q = 5$.

  (i) Write down a pair of simultaneous equations and solve them to find a and b.

Prepare for upcoming exams and tests using the **Assessment question** at the start of each chapter, and the **Assessment advice** throughout the chapter.

Assessment advice

- Practise the elimination method for solving simultaneous equations, especially when there are three equations. Common mistakes include forgetting to multiply the right-hand side as well as the left-hand side and failing to deal correctly with negative terms such as $-2y - (-7y)$ (which should equal 5y).
- The solution of equations (including simultaneous equations) can always be checked by substituting the answers back into the original equations.

Guided tour

Test Yourself questions throughout each chapter check your progress, as well as **worked examples**.

Worked example

Use Cramer's rule to find z in the system

$$\begin{pmatrix} 2 & 3 & -6 \\ 3 & 2 & -4 \\ 5 & -7 & 1 \end{pmatrix} \begin{pmatrix} x \\ y \\ z \end{pmatrix} = \begin{pmatrix} 13 \\ 0 \\ 0 \end{pmatrix}.$$

Solution

Cramer's rule gives

$$z = \frac{\begin{vmatrix} 2 & 3 & 13 \\ 3 & 2 & 0 \\ 5 & -7 & 0 \end{vmatrix}}{\begin{vmatrix} 2 & 3 & -6 \\ 3 & 2 & -4 \\ 5 & -7 & 1 \end{vmatrix}}.$$

The determinant on the bottom of this fraction has already been calculated to be 65 in the previous example.

Answer guidelines

Compare your responses with the **Answer guidelines** at the end of the chapter.

✱ Assessment question

Marks awarded on a course are known to be normally distributed with mean, μ, and standard deviation, σ. Based on these raw marks, degrees are classified as follows:

Marks	Degree classification
$x < 35$	Fail
$35 \le x < 45$	Third
$45 \le x < 56$	Lower second
$56 \le x < 73$	Upper second
$x \ge 73$	First

(a) If 8% of candidates are awarded first class degrees, show that $1.406\sigma + \mu = 73$.

If 5% fail the course, write down a second equation and hence determine the values of μ and σ, correct to two decimal places.

(b) Show that 40.4% of candidates are awarded upper-second class degrees.

(c) Use the binomial distribution to calculate the probability that in a group of 10 students, exactly half have upper-second class degrees.

(d) Comment on the validity of using the binomial model in part (c).

Check out the additional tips at the end of the chapter to approach and solve mathematical problems.

Approaching the question

- This question is in four parts. You need the answer to the first part in order to answer the second part.

- It helps to draw a diagram in part (a). You produce two equations in two unknowns that need to be solved.

Introduction

This book is intended to be used alongside your lecture notes, problem sheets and recommended textbooks.

The book splits naturally into two halves. The first six chapters cover the mathematics component of the course, and the last six cover the statistics component. Each half is free-standing so you can easily read the statistics chapters first if you wish.

Although the primary aim when writing this book was to produce a revision guide, we hope very much that it is not just a set of recipes that you need to follow to answer exam questions. While the length of the book necessarily means that the material is fairly concise, it does attempt to explain why you do things, as well as showing you what to do.

Learning mathematics and statistics should never be a passive activity, and this applies especially during revision. You will never become competent and confident in tackling exam questions unless you experience the success (and failure) of doing problems yourself. For this reason, there are many Test Yourself questions interspersed throughout the text, in addition to the more substantial Assessment Question that begins and ends each chapter. Fully worked solutions to every problem are provided on the companion website, but do make an honest attempt at each one before reading these.

The Assessment Question at the beginning of each chapter is probably longer than a real exam question. It more or less covers all of the material on that topic. Read through this question before you read the chapter. If you can answer the question and get it right, then there is probably less need for you to work through the relevant text in detail. On the other hand, if you cannot answer all of the Assessment Question you will need to revise this topic thoroughly. As you read the chapter and complete the exercises, you should find that you are gaining skills and knowledge that will enable you to answer the question. At the end of the chapter, please try the question again, using the hints provided, and then check your answers and working against those supplied on the website.

The online resources also contain many more exam-style questions and answers for you to try. These questions are of variable length, and are similar in style to those you will get in the real exam. There is also a batch of multiple-choice questions designed to test your knowledge. You might like to have a go at these first, as a sort of diagnostic test to help you identify your strengths and weaknesses.

1 Foundations

Topic map

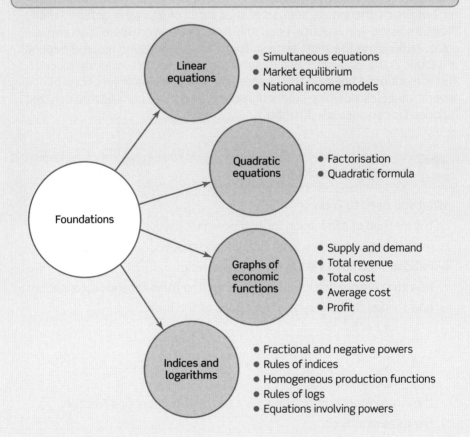

- **Foundations**

- **Linear equations**
  - Simultaneous equations
  - Market equilibrium
  - National income models

- **Quadratic equations**
  - Factorisation
  - Quadratic formula

- **Graphs of economic functions**
  - Supply and demand
  - Total revenue
  - Total cost
  - Average cost
  - Profit

- **Indices and logarithms**
  - Fractional and negative powers
  - Rules of indices
  - Homogeneous production functions
  - Rules of logs
  - Equations involving powers

A printable version of this topic map is available from **www.pearsoned.co.uk/econexpress**

Introduction

This chapter provides a quick survey of some important algebraic rules and techniques that are essential for any understanding of quantitative methods. Many economic relationships can be modelled using simple mathematical formulae and equations. These include linear equations, systems of linear equations involving two or three unknowns, quadratics and also equations involving unknown powers. Methods for solving all of these types of equation are described in the context of particular applications in finance, microeconomics and macroeconomics.

A *function of one variable* is a rule that assigns to any one incoming number a uniquely defined outgoing number. In economics these include cost, revenue and profit functions. Graphs of these functions are considered in this chapter, but the mathematical analysis of their rates of change is deferred until Chapters 3 and 4. In practice, economic functions involve more than two variables. Although in the short-term, output from a production process depends on labour, in the long-run it also depends on other factors including capital. This is mentioned briefly in this chapter, but the calculus of functions of several variables including production, utility and more complicated demand functions is considered in Chapter 5.

Revision checklist

What you need to know:

- ❑ the method of elimination for solving simultaneous linear equations;
- ❑ market equilibrium in supply and demand models;
- ❑ national income models in macroeconomics;
- ❑ how to solve quadratic equations using "the formula" and factorisation;
- ❑ how to sketch the graphs of functions of the form:
  - $y = ax + b$;
  - $y = \dfrac{a}{x} + b$;
  - $y = ax^2 + bx + c$;
- ❑ the interpretation of b^n when n is a negative number or a fraction;
- ❑ the rules of indices;
- ❑ homogeneous production functions;
- ❑ the definition of a logarithm and the rules of logarithms.

✳ Assessment advice

- Practise the elimination method for solving simultaneous equations, especially when there are three equations. Common mistakes include forgetting to multiply the right-hand side as well as the left-hand side and failing to deal correctly with negative terms such as $-2y - (-7y)$ (which should equal $5y$).

- The solution of equations (including simultaneous equations) can always be checked by substituting the answers back into the original equations.

- The discriminant $b^2 - 4ac$ is used to decide the number of roots of a quadratic. It can also be used to help you decide whether it is worthwhile trying to guess a possible factorisation. Unless the discriminant is a nice square number there is no point in trying to factorise, since the roots involve surds.

- If you are asked to sketch the graph of a function you are not expected to actually plot points accurately on graph paper. You just need to produce a graph of the correct shape and to identify key features including the intercepts with the axes.

- Although calculators can evaluate numbers involving powers and logs easily, it is worth learning what they represent. This is essential in order to interpret and make sense of algebraic expressions involving powers and logs.

- Learn the rules of indices and logs carefully. For example there is a rule for $\log_b(xy)$ but there is no rule for $\log_b(x + y)$.

✳ Assessment question

Could you answer this question? Guidelines on answering the question are presented at the end of this chapter.

A firm's fixed costs are 66 and the variable costs are 2 per unit. The corresponding profit function is $\pi = aQ^2 + bQ + c$.

(a) Write down expressions for the total and average cost functions, and sketch their graphs.

(b) Explain why $c = -66$.

(c) The firm makes a loss of 18 when $Q = 2$ and a profit of 24 when $Q = 5$.

    (i)   Write down a pair of simultaneous equations and solve them to find a and b.

(ii) Find the break-even points and hence sketch a graph of π against Q.

(iii) Find the maximum profit and the value of Q at which it is achieved.

(d) Use your answers to parts (a) and (c) to find an expression for total revenue and deduce the demand equation.

Linear equations

The equals symbol (=) is used in three different ways in mathematics. The expression $\pi = -2Q^2 + 15Q - 6$ provides a *formula* for profit, π, in terms of quantity, Q. Numerical values of Q can be substituted into the right-hand side to work out a value for the profit. The order in which the calculations are performed is governed by BIDMAS:

- brackets (first);
- indices (second);
- division and multiplication (a tie for third place);
- addition and subtraction (a tie for last place).

Operations of equal precedence (such as division and multiplication) are worked out from left to right. Substituting $Q = 3$ into the profit formula above gives:

$$\pi = -2 \times 3^2 + 15 \times 3 - 6$$
$$= -2 \times 9 + 15 \times 3 - 6 \text{ (indices)}$$
$$= -18 + 45 - 6 \text{ (multiplication)}$$
$$= 21 \text{ (addition and subtraction)}$$

The equals sign is also used for *identities* such as $(10 - 3Q)Q = 10Q - 3Q^2$. The expressions on either side of the equals sign produce the same value no matter what numerical value is used for the letter, Q. In fact, the above gives equivalent expressions for total revenue when the demand function is $P = 10 - 3Q$ as total revenue is given by PQ. There are occasions when it is convenient to use the factorised form, $(10 - 3Q)Q$, and others when it is better to use the expanded version, $10Q - 3Q^2$.

Finally, the equals sign is used in mathematical *equations* such as $2Q + 30 = 50$. This result is only true for one particular value of Q that needs to be found. This equation represents the problem of finding the output produced by a firm with supply equation $P = 2Q + 30$ when the market price is 50. Equations are solved by performing the same mathematical operation to both sides. In this case,

$2Q = 20$ (subtract 30 from both sides)

$Q = 10$ (divide both sides by 2)

In economics it is quite common to investigate problems where there are several equations and several unknowns.

Key definition

A market is in **equilibrium** when the quantities supplied and demanded are equal.

Worked example

The supply and demand functions for two interdependent commodities are given by the following:

$Q_{S_1} = -10 + P_1$

$Q_{S_2} = -5 + 6P_2$

$Q_{D_1} = 100 - 2P_1 + P_2$

$Q_{D_2} = 5 + 2P_1 - 3P_2$

where Q_{S_i}, Q_{D_i} and P_i denote the quantity supplied, quantity demanded and price of good i, respectively. Determine the equilibrium prices for this two-commodity model.

Solution

In this problem there are two goods whose demands are interrelated. The relation $Q_{D_1} = 100 - 2P_1 + P_2$ shows that, as expected, when the price of good 1 goes up, the demand for good 1 falls (since the coefficient of P_1 is negative). Also, since the coefficient of P_2 is positive, the demand for good 1 rises as the price of the alternative good goes up. This happens when the goods are *substitutable*; as the price of good 2 goes up consumers switch to good 1, provided it is an acceptable alternative.

In equilibrium, supply and demand are equal, so we can write $Q_{S_i} = Q_{D_i} = Q_i$. The equations become:

$Q_1 = -10 + P_1$

$Q_2 = -5 + 6P_2$

5

$$Q_1 = 100 - 2P_1 + P_2$$
$$Q_2 = 5 + 2P_1 - 3P_2$$

Hence $-10 + P_1 = 100 - 2P_1 + P_2$ (since both of these expressions are equal to Q_1), which can be rearranged as

$$3P_1 - P_2 = 110 \tag{1}$$

The same procedure applied to the other pair of equations gives

$$-2P_1 + 9P_2 = 10 \tag{2}$$

Equations 1 and 2 comprise a system of two *simultaneous equations* in two unknowns that can be solved by eliminating one of the unknowns. (Alternative methods using matrices are described in Chapter 6.)

In this case it is easier to eliminate P_2. This can be done by multiplying the first equation by nine and adding the second equation:

$$27P_1 - 9P_2 = 990$$
$$-2P_1 + 9P_2 = 10 \quad +$$
$$\overline{25P_1 \qquad = 1000}$$

Dividing both sides by 25 gives $P_1 = 40$. The equilibrium price of the second good is found by substituting the value of P_1 into either equation and solving for P_2. From the first equation,

$$120 - P_2 = 110$$
$$-P_2 = 10 \qquad \text{(subtract 120 from both sides)}$$
$$P_2 = 10 \qquad \text{(divide both sides by } -1)$$

Although not asked for in this question, the equilibrium quantities could be found by substituting the values of P_1 and P_2 into any of the original functions.

Test yourself

Q1. The supply and demand functions for two interdependent commodities are given by

$$Q_{S_1} = -6 + 2P_1$$
$$Q_{S_2} = -9 + 3P_2$$

$$Q_{D_1} = 79 - 5P_1 - P_2$$

$$Q_{D_2} = 86 - 2P_1 - 2P_2$$

where Q_{S_i}, Q_{J_i} and P_i denote the quantity supplied, quantity demanded and price of good i, respectively. Determine the equilibrium prices and quantities for this two-commodity model. Are the goods substitutable or complementary? Give a reason for your answer.

The previous example described how to solve a system of two equations. The elimination method can be extended to more complicated systems. For the simultaneous equations

$$2x - 2y + 3z = 7 \tag{1}$$

$$3x + 4y - 2z = 5 \tag{2}$$

$$-4x + 3y + 2z = 8 \tag{3}$$

there are three equations for three unknowns. The first equation is used to eliminate x from both the second and third equations.

Multiply (1) by 3, multiply (2) by 2 and subtract:

$$6x - 6y + 9z = 21$$
$$6x + 8y - 4z = 10 \qquad -$$
$$\overline{-14y + 13z = 11} \tag{4}$$

Multiply (1) by 2 and add (3):

$$4x - 4y + 6z = 14$$
$$-4x + 3y + 2z = 8 \qquad +$$
$$\overline{-y + 8z = 22} \tag{5}$$

Notice that (4) and (5) are a system of two equations in two unknowns. The variable y can be eliminated by multiplying (5) by 14 and subtracting from (4):

$$-14y + 13z = 11$$
$$-14y + 112z = 308 \qquad +$$
$$\overline{-99z = -297} \tag{6}$$

From Equation (6) we see that

$$z = \frac{-297}{-99} = 3.$$

7

Substituting this into (5) gives $-y + 24 = 22$, so $y = 2$.

Finally, substituting the values of y and z into (1) gives $2x + 5 = 7$, with solution $x = 1$.

The system has solution $x = 1$, $y = 2$, $z = 3$, which is checked easily by substituting these values back into the original three equations.

Test yourself

Q2. A factory produces three different models of car, A, B and C. The inputs required to produce one car of each type are given in the following table:

Resources	A	B	C
Materials	3	2	4
Energy	2	1	3
Labour	2	3	2

The number of units of materials, energy and labour available each day are 210, 145 and 145, respectively.

If x, y and z denote the daily production levels of cars for each model, write down a system of simultaneous equations, and solve this system to find x, y and z. You may assume that all resources are utilised fully each day.

The key result for analysing equilibrium in microeconomics is $Q_D = Q_S$, which applies to each good under consideration. The corresponding equation in macroeconomics is $Y = C + I$. The symbol Y (*national income*) is the flow of money received by households as payment for services. The symbol C (*consumption*) is the flow of money spent by households on goods supplied by firms. Firms also receive money due to *investment*, I. In equilibrium the flow of money into firms, $C + I$, balances the flow out of firms, Y. Once expressions (or values) are provided for C and I they can be substituted into the relation $Y = C + I$, and national income can be determined.

Suppose that the relationship between C and Y is $C = aY + b$. In this *consumption function*, a is the change in C brought about by a one-unit increase in Y, and is called the *marginal propensity to consume*. Households save the remaining income so a is between 0 and 1. The symbol b (*autonomous consumption*) is the consumption when there is no income. Let us also assume that investment is fixed at I^*. In equilibrium, $Y = C + I$ so

$$Y = aY + b + I^*,$$

which can be rearranged to give Y in terms of a, b and I^*:

$Y - aY = b + I^*$ (subtract aY from both sides)

$(1 - a)Y = b + I^*$ (take out a common factor of Y)

$$Y = \frac{b + I^*}{1 - a} \text{ (divide both sides by } 1 - a)$$

Not only does this result provide a formula that could be used to work out the value of national income, it can also be used to analyse the effect of making changes to a, b or I^*. Suppose that the investment rises by one unit to become $I^* + 1$. The new value of Y is

$$\frac{b + I^* + 1}{1 - a},$$

so the change in national income is

$$\frac{b + I^* + 1}{1 - a} - \frac{b + I^*}{1 - a} = \frac{b + I^* + 1 - b - I^*}{1 - a} = \frac{1}{1 - a}.$$

We know that $0 < a < 1$ so

$$\frac{1}{1 - a} > 1,$$

showing that the model predicts that the rise in national income is always greater than the rise in investment.

It is possible to solve models that include other sectors such as government activity. This is illustrated in the following example, in which G denotes government expenditure and Y_d denotes disposable income (income less tax, T).

Worked example

Calculate the equilibrium level of national income for the three-sector model:

$G = 30$ (government expenditure)

$I = 22$ (investment)

$C = 0.8Y_d + 100$ (consumption)

$T = 0.25Y + 15$ (taxation)

Solution

In addition to investment I, the flow of money to firms now includes government expenditure, G, so that in equilibrium, $Y = C + I + G$.

We are given specific numerical values for I and G so these can be substituted directly to give

$$Y = C + 22 + 30 = C + 52 \qquad\qquad (*)$$

Disposable income is the money households receive after the deduction of tax so

$$Y_d = Y - T = Y - (0.25Y + 15) = 0.75Y - 15.$$

The consumption function gives

$$C = 0.8Y_d + 100 = 0.8(0.75Y - 15) + 100 = 0.6Y + 88$$

From equation (*)

$$Y = (0.6Y + 88) + 52 = 0.6Y + 140$$

This can be solved easily to get $Y = 350$.

Test yourself

Q3. For a closed economy with no government intervention the consumption function is $C = 0.7Y + 20$ and planned investment $I = 40$. Calculate the equilibrium level of the following:

(a) national income;

(b) consumption;

(c) savings.

Q4. For the three-sector macroeconomic model:

$$I = I^*$$
$$G = G^*$$
$$T = tY + T^* \qquad (0 < t < 1, T^* > 0)$$
$$C = aY_d + b \qquad (0 < a < 1, b > 0)$$

show that the equilibrium level of national income is

$$Y = \frac{-aT^* + I^* + G^* + b}{1 - a + at}.$$

Hence find the change in national income when government expenditure rises by one unit.

Quadratic equations

Key definition

A quadratic equation takes the form $ax^2 + bx + c = 0$.

It is sometimes possible to solve quadratic equations using factorisation.

The quadratic $3x^2 - 4x$ has no constant term, and can be factorised easily by taking out a factor of x to give $x(3x - 4)$. Therefore, the equation $3x^2 - 4x = 0$ can be written as $x(3x - 4) = 0$. The only way that the product of two numbers is zero is when at least one of them is zero, so either $x = 0$ or $3x - 4 = 0$, so the two possible solutions are $x = 0$ and $x = 4/3$.

The quadratic $x^2 - 5x + 6$ can also be factorised. Two numbers that multiply to 6 and add up to −5 are −2 and −3 so $x^2 - 5x + 6$ can be expressed as $(x - 2)(x - 3)$. Therefore, the corresponding equation $x^2 - 5x + 6 = 0$ can be written as $(x - 2)(x - 3) = 0$ with solutions $x = 2$ and $x = 3$.

Unfortunately, not all quadratics can be factorised easily like this, so the preferred method is to use the formula

$$x = \frac{-b \pm \sqrt{b^2 - 4ac}}{2a}$$

where a, b and c are the coefficients of the x^2, x and constant terms, respectively.

Worked example

A firm's profit function is given by $\pi = -2Q^2 + 15Q - 6$. Find the quantities needed to produce a profit of 21 units.

Solution

Setting $\pi = 21$ gives $21 = -2Q^2 + 15Q - 6$. In order to be able to use the quadratic formula it is necessary to rearrange this into the form $aQ^2 + bQ + c = 0$. Putting all of the terms on the left-hand side gives

$$2Q^2 - 15Q + 27 = 0,$$

so $a = 2$, $b = -15$ and $c = 27$. Hence

$$Q = \frac{-(-15) \pm \sqrt{(-15)^2 - 4(2)(27)}}{2(2)} = \frac{15 \pm \sqrt{9}}{4} = \frac{15 \pm 3}{4}.$$

The two solutions are found by considering the + and − signs separately:

$$Q = \frac{15 + 3}{4} = 4.5$$

and

$$Q = \frac{15 - 3}{4} = 3.$$

All of the quadratics considered so far in this section have two solutions, which is not always the case. The number of solutions is determined by the sign of the *discriminant*, $b^2 - 4ac$.

- If $b^2 - 4ac > 0$ there are two solutions,

$$\frac{-b \pm \sqrt{b^2 - 4ac}}{2a}$$

- If $b^2 - 4ac = 0$ there is one solution,

$$\frac{-b \pm \sqrt{0}}{2a} = -\frac{b}{2a}$$

- If $b^2 - 4ac < 0$, there are no solutions because it is not possible to find the square root of a negative number.

Test yourself

Q5. A firm's supply and demand functions are:

$$P = Q_S^2 + Q_S + 14$$
$$P = -Q_D^2 - 5Q_D + 70$$

Calculate the market equilibrium price and quantity.

Graphs of economic functions

Key definitions

The general equation of a straight line is $y = mx + c$. The **gradient**, m, gives the change in y brought about by a one-unit increase in x; the **y-intercept**, c, is the y coordinate of the point where the line intersects the y-axis.

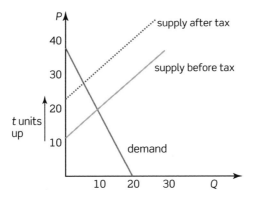

Figure 1.1

Figure 1.1 shows the graphs of the linear demand and supply functions

$$P = -2Q + 40$$

$$P = Q + 10$$

on the same axes. The demand function is sketched using the fact that it intersects the vertical axis at $P = 40$ and has a gradient of -2 so that for every 1 unit along, the graph goes down by 2 units. The supply function is sketched similarly. At the point of intersection supply and demand are equal, so the market equilibrium values of P and Q are 20 and 10, respectively.

Figure 1.1 also shows the new supply function after the imposition of a fixed tax, t. This is the amount of money that suppliers pass on to the government. The amount of money received by a firm falls to $P - t$ so the new supply function is $P = Q + 10 + t$. The effect is to keep the gradient unchanged but to increase the intercept by t so the line shifts up. Figure 1.1 shows that the point of intersection has moved both up and to the left. The effect of government taxation is to increase the equilibrium price and to decrease the corresponding quantity.

Key definitions

If FC and VC denote fixed and variable costs respectively, then

Total cost function, $TC = FC + (VC)Q$

Average cost function,

$$AC = \frac{TC}{Q}$$

Total revenue function, $TR = PQ$

Profit function, $\pi = TR - TC$

Worked example

If fixed costs are 48, variable costs per unit are 4 and the demand function is $P = 32 - 2Q$, sketch the graphs of each of the following economic functions:

(a) total cost;

(b) average cost;

(c) total revenue;

(d) profit.

Solution

(a) $TC = FC + (VC)Q = 48 + 4Q$.

The graph is a straight line with intercept 48 and gradient 4, and is sketched in Figure 1.2.

(b) $AC = \dfrac{TC}{Q} = \dfrac{48 + 4Q}{Q} = \dfrac{48}{Q} + 4$.

The graph is an L-shaped curve, shown in Figure 1.3. It can be sketched either from a table of values or by noting that the first term, $48/Q$

- increases without bound as Q approaches zero;

- decreases to zero as Q increases so that AC approaches 4.

(c) $TR = PQ = (32 - 2Q)Q = 32Q - 2Q^2$.

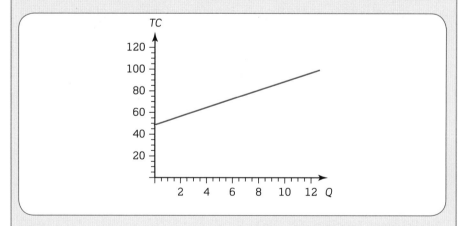

Figure 1.2

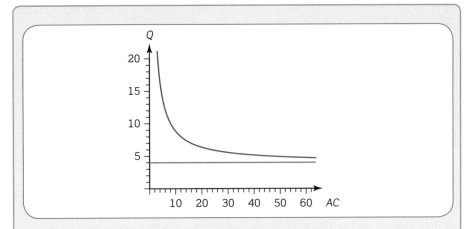

Figure 1.3

The graph is an inverted U-shaped curve, shown in Figure 1.4. It can be sketched either from a table of values or by noting that

- the coefficient of Q^2 is negative so the curve bends downwards at its ends;
- the factorisation $(32 - 2Q)Q$ shows that the curve crosses the Q-axis at $Q = 0$ and $Q = 16$;
- by symmetry, the maximum point on the graph occurs halfway between 0 and 16, at $Q = 8$, which gives a total revenue of 128.

(d) $\pi = TR - TC = (32Q - 2Q^2) - 48 + 4Q = -2Q^2 + 28Q - 48$.

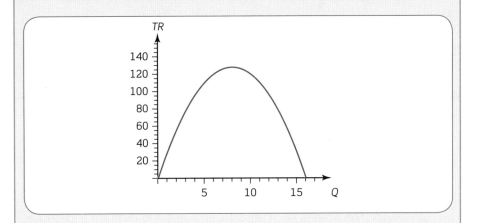

Figure 1.4

The graph is an inverted U-shaped curve, shown in Figure 1.5. It can be sketched either from a table of values or by noting that

- the coefficient of Q^2 is negative so the curve bends downwards at its ends;
- the factorisation $-2(Q^2 - 14Q + 24) = -2(Q - 2)(Q - 12)$ shows that the curve crosses the Q-axis at $Q = 2$ and $Q = 12$. These are the break-even points and they can also be found by solving the equation $Q^2 - 14Q + 24 = 0$ using the quadratic formula, which gives

$$\frac{-(-14) \pm \sqrt{(-14)^2 - 4 \times 1 \times 24}}{2 \times 1} = \frac{14 \pm 10}{2} = 2, 12;$$

- the graph crosses the vertical axis when $Q = 0$, which gives $\pi = -48$;
- by symmetry: the maximum point on the graph occurs halfway between 2 and 12, at $Q = 7$, which gives a profit of 50.

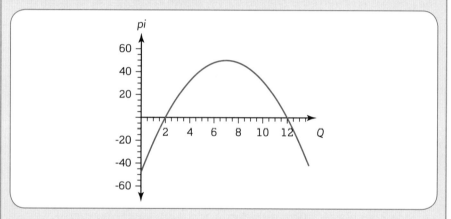

Figure 1.5

Q6. The total revenue and average cost functions are given by

$$TR = 10Q - Q^2 \text{ and } AC = \frac{12}{Q} + 2$$

(a) Write down an expression for the total cost function, TC, and hence state the fixed cost and variable cost per unit.

(b) Sketch the graphs of TC and TR on the same diagram and hence estimate the break-even values of Q.

Indices and logarithms

Key definitions

A number written as b^n is said to be in **exponential form**: the positive number b is called the **base** and the number n is called the **power, index** or **exponent**.

Numbers written in exponential form with a zero, negative or fractional index are interpreted as follows:

- $b^0 = 1$ (any number raised to the power of zero is one);
- $b^{-n} = 1/b^n$ (negative powers indicate reciprocals);
- $b^{1/n} = \sqrt[n]{b}$ (fractional powers indicate roots);

which give $5^0 = 1$, $7^{-2} = 1/7^2 = 1/49$ and $81^{1/4} = \sqrt[4]{81} = 3$, respectively. For more complicated indices we proceed in stages. For example, to evaluate $8^{-4/3}$ we could work as follows:

$$8^{-4/3} = (8^{\frac{1}{3}})^{-4} = 2^{-4} \text{ (the index 1/3 denotes cube roots)}$$

$$= \frac{1}{2^4} \text{ (the negative index denotes reciprocals)}$$

$$= \frac{1}{16} \; (2^4 = 2 \times 2 \times 2 \times 2 = 16).$$

Numbers written in exponential form can be simplified according to the following rules:

- **Rule 1** $b^m \times b^n = b^{m+n}$ (when you multiply, you add the powers)
- **Rule 2** $\dfrac{b^m}{b^n} = b^{m-n}$ (when you divide, you subtract the powers)
- **Rule 3** $(b^m)^n = b^{mn}$ (when you take a power of a power, you multiply the powers)
- **Rule 4** $(ab)^n = a^n b^n$ (you can apply the power to each term separately in a product)

One useful application of these rules concerns production functions. The output, Q, from a production process depends on a variety of inputs including capital, K, and labour, L. For example, the function might be $Q = 30K^{\frac{1}{2}}L^{\frac{1}{4}}$. If the inputs are known then this formula can be used to work out the corresponding output. If $K = 36$ and $L = 16$ then $Q = 30 \times 36^{\frac{1}{2}} \times 16^{\frac{1}{4}} = 30 \times 6 \times 2 = 360$ (because $36^{\frac{1}{2}} = \sqrt{36} = 6$ and $16^{\frac{1}{4}} = \sqrt[4]{16} = 2$).

We can also analyse the effect of scaling the inputs. If the values of K and L both double, does the output also double, or does it go up by more or less than this? This question is answered easily. Starting with $Q = 30K^{\frac{1}{2}}L^{\frac{1}{4}}$, we replace K by $2K$ and L by $2L$ to obtain

$$30(2K)^{\frac{1}{2}}(2L)^{\frac{1}{4}} = 30 \times 2^{\frac{1}{2}} \times K^{\frac{1}{2}} \times 2^{\frac{1}{4}} \times L^{\frac{1}{4}} \text{ (using the fourth rule of indices)}$$

$$= 30 \times 2^{\frac{3}{4}} \times K^{\frac{1}{2}} \times L^{\frac{1}{2}} \text{ (using the first rule of indices)}$$

$$= 2^{\frac{3}{4}}Q \text{ (because } Q = 30K^{\frac{1}{2}}L^{\frac{1}{4}}\text{)}.$$

This is less than double since $\dfrac{3}{4} < 1$. (In fact, $2^{\frac{3}{4}} \approx 1.68$.) This argument applies to any scaling of the inputs. If K and L both get multiplied by λ (the Greek letter lambda), it is easy to see that Q gets scaled by $\lambda^{\frac{3}{4}}$ (which is less than λ since $\dfrac{3}{4} < 1$).

Key definition

A production function, $Q = f(K, L)$, is **homogeneous of degree n** if $f(\lambda K, \lambda L) = \lambda^n f(K, L)$.

The function is said to display **decreasing, constant** or **increasing returns to scale** when $n < 1$, $n = 1$ and $n > 1$, respectively.

From this definition, the production function, $Q = 30K^{\frac{1}{2}}L^{\frac{1}{4}}$, considered above is therefore homogeneous of degree 3/4 with decreasing returns to scale.

Test yourself

Q7. For each of the following production functions,
  (a) calculate the output when $K = 27$ and $L = 8$;
  (b) show that they are homogeneous and comment on their returns to scale.
  (i) $Q = 100K^{\frac{1}{3}}L^{\frac{2}{3}}$
  (ii) $Q = 10KL + 0.2L^2$

The process of going backwards and expressing a number in exponential form occurs sufficiently frequently to warrant its own notation and terminology.

Key definition

If a number $M = b^n$, we say that n is the **logarithm of M to base b** and write $n = \log_b M$.

For example,

$\log_{10} 1000 = 3$ (because $1000 = 10^3$)

$$\log_5 \frac{1}{25} = -2 \ \left(\text{because} \frac{1}{25} = 5^{-2}\right)$$

$$\log_9 3 = \frac{1}{2} \ \left(\text{because } 3 = \sqrt{9} = 9^{\frac{1}{2}}\right)$$

Given that logarithms are just another way of writing down an index they can be manipulated using the following three rules, which are analogous to the rules considered previously for powers:

> - **Rule 1** $\log_b(xy) = \log_b x + \log_b y$
> - **Rule 2**
>
> $$\log_b\left(\frac{x}{y}\right) = \log_b x - \log_b y$$
>
> - **Rule 3** $\log_b x^n = n \log_b x$

These rules can be used to "expand" a logarithm:

$$\log_b\left(\frac{x^2 y^3}{z^4}\right) = \log_b x^2 + \log_b y^3 - \log_b z^4 \text{ (first and second rules)}$$

$$= 2 \log_b x + 3 \log_b y - 4 \log_b z \text{ (third rule)}$$

and also to express a string of terms as a single logarithm:

$$3 \log_b u + \frac{1}{2} \log_b v - \log_b w = \log_b u^3 + \log_b v^{\frac{1}{2}} - \log_b w \text{ (third rule)}$$

$$= \log_b\left(\frac{u^3 \sqrt{v}}{w}\right) \text{ (first and second rules)}$$

Logarithms can be used to solve equations in which the unknown appears as a power, such as the equation $1000 \times 1.05^n = 1800$. This equation represents a problem in finance in which £1,000 is invested at 5% compound interest. The number n denotes the number of years needed for this investment to increase to £1,800. Dividing both sides by 1,000 gives

$$1.05^n = 1.8$$

$$\log 1.05^n = \log 1.8 \ \text{(take logs of both sides)}$$

$$n \log 1.05 = \log 1.8 \ \text{(third rule)}$$

$$n = \frac{\log 1.8}{\log 1.05} \text{(divide both sides by log 1.05)}$$

$$= \frac{0.2552725051}{0.02118929907} = 12.05$$

(the button labelled log on a calculator works out the logarithm to base 10) .

In the context of annual compounding, this shows that after 12 years the amount will not quite have reached 1,800 (in fact $1000 \times 1.05^{12} = 1795.86$), so it would take an extra year before the target figure is achieved.

Test yourself

Q8.

(a) Write down the values of $\log_b b^4$, $\log_b \sqrt{b}$, $\log_b \dfrac{1}{b}$, $\log_b 1$.

(b) Express as a single logarithm, $4 \log_b x + 2 \log_b y - 3 \log_b z$.

(c) By taking logarithms of both sides of the equation $3^x = 2 \times 4^x$, find the value of x correct to three decimal places.

Chapter summary – pulling it all together

By the end of this chapter you should be able to:

	Confident ✓	Not confident?
Solve systems of two linear equations in two unknowns		Revise pages 5–7
Solve systems of three linear equations in three unknowns		Revise pages 7–8
Solve national income determination models		Revise pages 8–10
Use the formula for solving quadratic equations		Revise pages 11–12
Know the key features of the graphs of linear, quadratic and reciprocal functions		Revise pages 12–16
Derive expressions for total revenue, total cost, average cost and profit functions		Revise pages 13–16
Know the meaning of b^n and use the rules of indices		Revise pages 17–18
Understand what a logarithm is and use the rules of logs		Revise pages 18–20

Now try the assessment question at the start of the chapter using the answer guidelines below.

Answer guidelines

✳ Assessment question

A firm's fixed costs are 66 and the variable costs are 2 per unit. The corresponding profit function is $\pi = aQ^2 + bQ + c$.

(a) Write down expressions for the total and average cost functions and sketch their graphs.

(b) Explain why $c = -66$.

(c) The firm makes a loss of 18 when $Q = 2$ and a profit of 24 when $Q = 5$.

    (i) Write down a pair of simultaneous equations and solve them to find a and b.

    (ii) Find the break-even points and hence sketch a graph of π against Q.

    (iii) Find the maximum profit and the value of Q at which it is achieved.

(d) Use your answers to parts (a) and (c) to find an expression for total revenue and deduce the demand equation.

Approaching the question

- This question is in four parts, which are linked.
- Decide at the beginning exactly what individual steps are needed to tackle each part.
- In parts (b) and (c) you are told that the profit function is a quadratic and you need to find the values of the three coefficients using the information provided. Once these have been determined you need to sketch the graph using the standard procedure outlined in the text.
- The profit function is usually found from known expressions for TR and TC using the relation $\pi = TR - TC$. In the last part of the question you work backwards. You have already obtained expressions for π and TC in earlier parts of the question, so you can deduce TR.

Method of solution

- Part (a) of the question is very easy and is similar to the first parts of the worked example on page 14.
- Part (b) requires a bit more thought. The number 66 is obviously the fixed costs in this question. You need to give a mathematical reason

why the negative of this value appears as the constant term in the profit function. Hint: what can you say about profit when $Q = 0$?

- To tackle part (c), you need first to write down the equations. To do this just substitute $Q = 2$ and $Q = 5$ into the general expression for π. Note that a loss of 18 corresponds to a profit of −18. No method is specified for the solution of the system of equations so you can use the elimination method or use matrix methods (described in Chapter 6). Once the values of a and b have been found, you can use factorisation or the quadratic formula to find the break-even values of Q, and hence sketch the graph. You are not expected to actually plot points in this type of question. You must, however, indicate the key points on the sketch, which are the points where the graph crosses both axes, together with the coordinates of the maximum point on the curve.

- The formula for profit, $\pi = TR - TC$, can be rearranged to give $TR = \pi + TC$. Expressions for TC and π have already been obtained in parts (a) and (c) so these can be used to find TR.

- The formula for total revenue, $TR = PQ$, can be rearranged to give $P = TR/Q$ so the demand function can be deduced easily from the expression for total revenue.

Companion website

Go to the companion website at **www.pearsoned.co.uk/econexpress** to find more revision support online for this topic area.

Notes

Notes

2 Financial mathematics

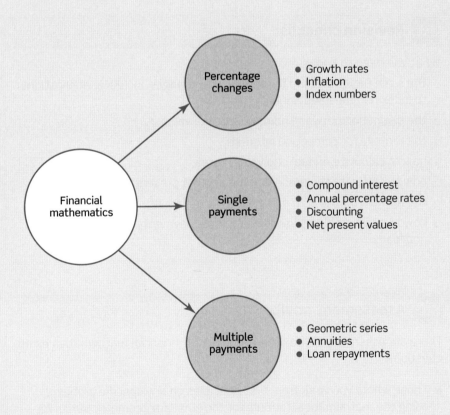

- Percentage changes
  - Growth rates
  - Inflation
  - Index numbers

- Financial mathematics

- Single payments
  - Compound interest
  - Annual percentage rates
  - Discounting
  - Net present values

- Multiple payments
  - Geometric series
  - Annuities
  - Loan repayments

A printable version of this topic map is available from **www.pearsoned.co.uk/econexpress**

Introduction

In this chapter we revise work on percentages, and consider applications in finance. The use of the scale factor method provides a quick way of handling percentage change calculations, and is invaluable for reverse percentage problems. The use of index numbers enables us to spot trends in time series, and monetary values can be adjusted to take inflation into account.

The majority of savings and loan facilities use compound interest, although the interest might be added more than once a year. If a single deposit is saved in a bank account, it is easy to work out the future value by repeatedly multiplying this amount by the relevant scale factor. However, if a regular series of savings (or repayments for a loan) are made, it is necessary to use the formula for the sum of a geometric series to perform the calculations efficiently.

 ## Revision checklist

What you need to know:

- ❏ the scale factor method for percentage changes, including applications to index numbers and annual growth;
- ❏ the distinction between nominal and real values;
- ❏ the formula for compound interest;
- ❏ how to calculate annual equivalent rates;
- ❏ how to calculate the present value and net present value;
- ❏ the formula for the sum of a geometric series;
- ❏ how to solve problems involving multiple payments, including annuities and loans.

✳ Assessment advice

There are essentially three different styles of financial mathematics exam questions:

- Those where you work from first principles on any specific problem, using the mathematical formula for the sum of a geometric series for multiple payment problems.
- Those where you are allowed to quote formulae for each type of problem, and then just substitute in specific values for the letters.

- Those where you are *given* the formula in the question, and you just substitute in the numbers.

Make sure that you know exactly what is expected on your course, so that you can target your revision accordingly. Obviously the easiest of the three is the last one, but even here you should be aware of where the formula comes from, so that you can adapt it to any situation.

 Assessment question

Could you answer this question? Guidelines on answering the question are presented at the end of this chapter.

(a) Country A has twice the GDP of country B. In the future, the annual growth rates of these two countries are expected to be 2% and 6%, respectively. After how many years will the GDP of country B exceed that of country A?

(b) The sum of £4,000 is borrowed from a bank, at a rate of 4.8% interest, compounded monthly. The loan is repaid in monthly instalments of £x. Find an expression, in terms of x, for the outstanding debt at the end of n months.

    (i)   How many months would it take to repay the loan if $x = £100$?

    (ii) What should the monthly repayment be if the debt is to be cleared after 18 months?

    (iii) Describe what happens to the debt when the monthly repayment is £16.

Percentage changes

The word "percentage" literally means "per hundredth", so r% of a quantity P is

$$P \times \frac{r}{100}.$$

If P increases by r% then we end up with the original amount, P, together with the extra

$$P \times \frac{r}{100},$$

giving a final amount:

$$P + P \times \frac{r}{100} = P\left(1 + \frac{r}{100}\right).$$

The number

$$1 + \frac{r}{100}$$

is called the *scale factor*, and is the number you multiply by to work out the final value after the increase.

Worked example

A company awards each of its employees a 3% annual pay rise.

(a) Calculate the salary after the increase for someone currently earning £28,000.

(b) Calculate the current salary of someone who earns £46,350 after the increase.

The following year the company again awards a uniform pay increase for each employee and, as a result, one person's salary rises from £18,000 to £18,450.

(c) Find the firm's percentage pay rise for the second year.

(d) Calculate the overall percentage growth in salary for the 2-year period.

Solution

(a) For a percentage increase of 3% the scale factor is 1.03. To work out the final salary *after* the increase we *multiply* by this scale factor to get $28{,}000 \times 1.03 = £28{,}840$.

(b) To go backwards, and find the original salary *before* the increase, we *divide* by the scale factor to get $46{,}350 \div 1.03 = £45{,}000$.

(c) The scale factor for the second year's pay rise is

$$\frac{18450}{18000} = 1.025 = 1 + \frac{2.5}{100},$$

which represents an increase of 2.5%.

(d) During the first year, someone's salary gets multiplied by 1.03; during the second year, this gets multiplied by 1.025. So the overall effect is to multiply by

$$1.03 \times 1.025 = 1.05575 = 1 + \frac{5.575}{100},$$

which represents an increase of 5.575%. Notice that this is not the same as the sum of the individual rises. This is because during the second year, the 2.5% increase applies not only to the original salary, but also to the increase accrued during the first year.

Test yourself

Q1. China's GDP per capita (measured in US dollars) in 2009 and 2010 was $3,749 and $4,433, respectively.*

(a) Calculate the percentage increase.

(b) Calculate China's GDP in 2011 if it grows by a further 22.83% during this year.

(c) Calculate the overall percentage growth during this 2-year period.

*Source: World Bank, **http://data.worldbank.org**.

We now describe two applications of the scale factor method:

- inflation;
- index numbers.

Inflation

Economic data often take the form of a *time series* where various economic indicators are published on an annual, quarterly or monthly basis. These might include output, national debt and energy prices. Unfortunately, it is quite difficult to interpret trends in these figures when general prices are rising anyway due to inflation. The preferred measure of inflation is the *Consumers' Prices Index* (CPI) which is based on the average prices of a preselected basket of consumer goods and services, weighted according to their importance. Economists handle this situation by distinguishing between *nominal* and *real* data. Nominal data are the original raw figures whereas real data have been adjusted to take inflation into account.

Table 2.1 shows the August figures for the CPI for three consecutive years, together with the average house prices in August between 2009 and 2012.

These nominal figures suggest that there was quite a big increase in prices in 2010 followed by a fall almost back to the original levels. However, a different picture emerges when the prices are adjusted to "2009 prices". In 2011 the average house price was £161,982. During the previous 12 months inflation was 4.5% with a scale factor of 1.045, so the "2010 price" is 161,982 ÷ 1.045 = £155,007. To backtrack to "2009 prices" we divide again, this time by 1.031, to get £150,346. Similar adjustments can be made to the house prices in 2010 and 2012. These are shown in Table 2.2, which shows quite clearly that house prices fell in real terms, and that even the gain in 2010 was quite modest.

Table 2.1

Year	2009	2010	2011	2012
CPI		3.1%	4.5%	2.5%
House prices*	£160,947	£168,388	£161,982	£160,142

*Source: Halifax House Price Index, **www.lloydsbankgroup.com**.

Table 2.2

Year	2009	2010	2011	2012
2009 prices	£160,947	£163,325	£150,346	£145,013

Test yourself

Q2. Use the information provided in Table 2.1 to produce a table of house prices adjusted to "2010 prices".

Index numbers

It may not be easy to identify trends in time series when the numbers involved are large, and it can be equally difficult to compare two series when the numbers are of different orders of magnitude. To avoid this difficulty, it is helpful to replace the original data by index numbers. One time period (usually, but not always, the first) is chosen as the base period and allocated the index 100. The index numbers of the other periods are then calculated by working out the scale factor from the base period to the new period and multiplying by 100.

Table 2.3 gives the number of people (in thousands) who were unemployed in the USA during the period 2005–11. The index numbers are shown in the bottom row. The base year is 2005. The index number associated with 2006 is calculated as follows:

$$\frac{7001}{7591} \times 100 = 92.$$

This shows that there was an 8% fall in unemployment during 2006. On the other hand, the index number for 2010 was 195, indicating a 95% increase between 2005 and 2010.

Table 2.3

Year	2005	2006	2007	2008	2009	2010	2011
Number unemployed*	7,591	7,001	7,078	8,924	14,265	14,825	13,747
Index number	100	92	93	118	188	195	181

*Source: Bureau of Labour Statistics, http://data.bls.gov.

Test yourself

Q3. Table 2.4 shows the index numbers associated with a price of wheat during the first six months of 2013.

Table 2.4

Month	Jan	Feb	Mar	Apr	May	June
Index	94	97	100	98	105	110

(a) Which month is chosen as the base month?

(b) What is the percentage change in price from March to June?

(c) What is the percentage change in price from January to May?

(d) What, if anything, does this series indicate about the underlying trend in wheat prices?

Single payments

For *compound interest*, instead of receiving a fixed amount of interest each year, based on the original investment, you also get interest on any previous interest. The original amount of money is called the *principal*, P, and the final sum is called the *future value*, S. If the interest is compounded at an annual rate of r%, then every year the investment gets multiplied by the scale factor, $1 + \dfrac{r}{100}$, so that, after n years, the future value is given by the formula:

$$S = P\left(1 + \frac{r}{100}\right)^n.$$

Sometimes the principal is compounded more than once a year. The following example shows how to calculate future values in this situation.

Worked example

A principal of £10,000 is invested at 6% interest for 2 years.

(a) Find the future value if the interest is compounded:
  (i) annually;
  (ii) semi-annually;
  (iii) monthly.
(b) Calculate the annual equivalent rate (AER) for (ii) and (iii) in part (a).

Solution

(a) (i) If the interest is compounded annually, then each year the principal gets scaled by 1.06, so the future value after 2 years is $10{,}000 \times 1.06^2 = £11{,}236.00$.

  (ii) If the interest is compounded semi-annually, then an interest of $6 \div 2 = 3\%$ is added on every 6 months; because there are four 6-month periods in 2 years, the future value is $10{,}000 \times (1.03)^4 = £11{,}255.09$.

  (iii) If the interest is compounded monthly, then an interest of $6/12 = 0.5\%$ is added on every month; because there are 24 months in 2 years, the future value is $10{,}000 \times 1.005^{24} = £11{,}271.60$.

(b)   The *annual equivalent rate* is the rate of interest that, when compounded annually, produces the same yield as the stated rate of interest.

(ii) For semi-annual compounding a principal gets multiplied by 1.03^2 during the course of a year. Under annual compounding, with a rate of $r\%$, the scale factor is

$$1 + \frac{r}{100}.$$

If these are to be equivalent then

$$1 + \frac{r}{100} = 1.03^2 = 1.0609,$$

which gives an AER of 6.09%.

(iii) For monthly compounding,

$$1 + \frac{r}{100} = 1.005^{12} = 1.0617,$$

which gives an AER of 6.17%.

In general, the formula for compounding is

$$S = P\left(1 + \frac{r}{100k}\right)^{kn}$$

where k is the number of compounding periods in a year.

The worked example shows that, as expected, the future value rises as the frequency of compounding increases. If the number of compounding periods increases indefinitely, the future values eventually settle down to a particular value. This is referred to as *continuous compounding*, and is described in Chapter 4.

Test yourself

Q4. A principal of £5,000 is invested at 4% interest for 3 years. If the interest is compounded quarterly, find the

(i) future value;

(ii) annual equivalent rate.

It often happens that we know what we would like the future value to be, and work backwards to find the amount we need to invest today to achieve this goal.

Key definitions

The process of working backwards in time to find the original principal from a future value is called **discounting**, and the rate of interest is then referred to as the **discount rate**.

The amount that is invested initially to produce a specified future value after a fixed period of time is called the **present value**, and the present value of a revenue flow minus the original cost is the **net present value (NPV)**.

These terms are illustrated in the following example.

Worked example

(a) Find the present value of £400 in 5 years' time if the discount rate is 3.4%, compounded semi-annually.

(b) A project requiring an initial outlay of £60,000 is expected to produce a return of £65,000 in 3 years' time. If the prevailing market rate is 3% compounded annually, calculate the NPV and hence decide whether this investment is worthwhile.

Solution

(a) The formula for compound interest,

$$S = P\left(1 + \frac{r}{100k}\right)^{kn}$$

can easily be rearranged to express P in terms of S by dividing both sides by the term in the brackets to give

$$P = S\left(1 + \frac{r}{100k}\right)^{-kn}$$

where the negative power is used to denote a reciprocal.

In this case, $S = 400$, $r = 3.4$, $k = 2$ and $n = 5$, so the present value is $P = 400 \times (1.017)^{-10} = £337.95$.

This is the amount you would need to invest now if it is to grow to £400 in 5 years' time.

(b) In this case, $S = 65,000$, $r = 3$, $k = 1$ and $n = 3$, so the present value is $P = 65,000 \times (1.03)^{-3} = £59,484.21$, giving an NPV of $59,484.21 - 60,000 = -£515.79$.

The fact that the NPV is negative indicates that the project is not worthwhile. You would be better off just investing the £60,000 at the market rate.

Test yourself

Q5. (a) If the discount rate is 7%, compounded annually, find the present value of

(i) £30,000 in 3 years' time;

(ii) £50,000 in 4 years' time.

(b) A project requires an initial investment of £58,000, and is guaranteed to provide a return of £30,000 after 3 years and a further £50,000 after 4 years. Use your answers to part (a) to calculate the NPV, if the discount rate is 7% compounded annually. Is the investment worthwhile?

Multiple payments

In practice, people often save the same amount of money on a regular basis. For example, someone might choose to save £250 at the beginning of each month for 2 years. If the account offers a return of 3.6%, compounded monthly, then the future value of the first payment is $250(1.003)^{24}$, since this sum is invested for 24 months at a rate of $3.6/12 = 0.3\%$ per month. The second payment is invested for 23 months, so its future value is $250(1.003)^{23}$, and so on. The last payment is only invested for 1 month, and the total investment at the end of the 2-year period is $250(1.003)^{24} + 250(1.003)^{23} + \ldots + 250(1.003)$, which can be rewritten in ascending powers as $250(1.003) + 250(1.003)^2 + \ldots + 250(1.003)^{24}$.

The first term is $250(1.003)$, and subsequent terms are formed by multiplying by 1.003 each time. We could, of course, evaluate this series by working out each of the 24 terms and adding together. However, this is an example of a geometric series, and there is a special formula that can be used for its sum.

Key definitions

A sequence of numbers in which you multiply by a fixed number to go from one term to the next is called a **geometric progression**, and the multiplier is called a **geometric ratio**. The series obtained by summing consecutive terms in such a sequence is called a **geometric series**.

If the first term in a geometric series is a and the geometric ratio is r, then the sum of the first n terms of the series can be found using the formula

$$a\left(\frac{r^n - 1}{r - 1}\right).$$

This formula can be used to work out the sum of the series
$250(1.003) + 250(1.003)^2 + \ldots + 250(1.003)^{24}$ by substituting
$a = 250(1.003)$, $r = 1.003$ and $n = 24$ to get

$$250(1.003)\left(\frac{1.003^{24} - 1}{1.003 - 1}\right) = £6230.26.$$

If the money was saved over a period of n years, then the total saved would be

$$250(1.003)\left(\frac{1.003^n - 1}{1.003 - 1}\right).$$

This expression can be used to determine the number of months needed to save a designated amount of money. For example, if the target figure is £10,000 then n satisfies the equation

$$250(1.003)\left(\frac{1.003^n - 1}{1.003 - 1}\right) = 10,000,$$

which can be rearranged as

$$1.003^n = 1 + \frac{10,000(1.003 - 1)}{250(1.003)} = 1.11964.$$

This can be solved by taking logs of both sides:

$$\log(1.003)^n = \log(1.11964)$$

$$n \log(1.003) = \log(1.11964)$$

$$n = \frac{\log(1.11964)}{\log(1.003)} = 37.7.$$

So it would take 38 months to save £10,000.

Test yourself

Q6. At the beginning of a year, an amount of £P is invested and earns interest at a rate of r% compounded annually. At the end of each year, an additional investment of £Q is put into the fund. Show that the amount invested at the end of n years is

$$P(1 + r/100)^n + \frac{Q(1 + r/100)^n - Q}{r/100}.$$

On 1 January 2013, I have £2,000 in my bank account, which offers a return of 5% compounded annually. I decide to save a fixed amount at the end of every year, starting on 31 December 2013. I would like to use these savings to put down a £60,000 deposit on a house, which I hope to buy at the beginning of 2020. How much do I need to save each year?

The following worked examples show how to use the formula for the sum of a geometric series to work out the

- present value of an annuity;
- monthly repayments of a loan.

Annuities

Worked example

Find the present value of an annuity that provides an annual income of £8,000 at the end every year for the next 10 years, assuming that the interest rate is fixed at an agreed rate of 6% compounded annually. How much money would need to be invested now if the income is to be provided in perpetuity?

Solution

An *annuity* is a sequence of regular equal payments that are paid out in the future. The present value is the value of the lump sum that needs to be invested now to provide for these payments. It can be worked out by summing the present values of the individual payments.

The first payment of £8,000 is paid at the end of the first year so its present value is $8{,}000(1.06)^{-1}$. The present value of the second payment is $8{,}000(1.06)^{-2}$, and the last payment has a present value of $8{,}000(1.06)^{-10}$. The total present value is $8{,}000(1.06)^{-1} + 8{,}000(1.06)^{-2} + \ldots + 8{,}000(1.06)^{-10}$, which is the sum of a geometric series with $n = 10$, $a = 8{,}000(1.06)^{-1}$ and $r = (1.06)^{-1}$. The formula for the sum gives

$$8{,}000(1.06)^{-1}\left(\frac{(1.06)^{-10} - 1}{(1.06)^{-1} - 1}\right) = £58{,}880.70.$$

If the payments are to last n years then the present value would be

$$8{,}000(1.06)^{-1}\left(\frac{(1.06)^{-n} - 1}{(1.06)^{-1} - 1}\right).$$

Notice that the number $(1.06)^{-n}$ is the same as

$$\frac{1}{1.06^{n}},$$

which gets ever closer to zero as n increases. So if the fund is to pay out £8,000 a year, for ever, then today's investment needs to be

$$8{,}000(1.06)^{-1}\left(\frac{0 - 1}{(1.06)^{-1} - 1}\right) = £133{,}333.33.$$

The general formula for the present value, A, of an annuity that pays out £R at the end of every year for n years, when the interest rate is r% compounded annually, is

$$A = R(1 + r/100)^{-1}\left[\frac{(1 + r/100)^{-n} - 1}{(1 + r/100)^{-1} - 1}\right],$$

which can be rewritten as

$$A = R\left[\frac{(1 + r/100)^n - 1}{(r/100)(1 + r/100)^n}\right].$$

If the annuity is to last in perpetuity then

$$A = \frac{100R}{r}.$$

Test yourself

Q7. A generous quantitative methods lecturer decides to donate a sum of money so that an annual prize of £500 may be awarded every year for 15 years to the student who scores the highest mark on the exam paper. How much needs to be invested now if the first prize is to be awarded exactly 1 year from now, and the annual interest rate is 5.4%?

Loan repayments

Worked example

Calculate the monthly repayments needed to repay a £200,000 loan that is paid back over 25 years, when the interest rate is 6% compounded annually.

Solution

During the first year two things happen. First, the bank charges 6% interest on the loan so the debt rises to 200,000(1.06). Second, the debt reduces by 12x where x denotes the monthly repayment. The outstanding debt at the end of the first year is 200,000(1.06) − 12x.

During the second year the same things happen. The debt gets scaled by 1.06, and the monthly repayments reduce the debt by 12x. The outstanding debt at the end of the second year is

$$(200{,}000(1.06) - 12x)(1.06) - 12x = 200{,}000(1.06)^2 - 12x(1.06) - 12x.$$

The pattern is repeated every year, so after 25 years the outstanding debt is

$$200{,}000(1.06)^{25} - 12x(1.06)^{24} - 12x(1.06)^{23} - \ldots - 12x$$

$$= 200{,}000(1.06)^{25} - 12x(1 + 1.06 + 1.06^2 + \ldots + 1.06^{24})$$

$$= 20{,}000(1.06)^{25} - 12x\left(\frac{1.06^{25} - 1}{1.06 - 1}\right)$$

$$= 858{,}374.14 - 658.37x.$$

The value of x is chosen to ensure that the debt is paid off at the end of 25 years, so the monthly repayment needs to be

$$x = \frac{858{,}374.14}{658.37} = £1303.79.$$

In general, if an amount £A, is borrowed at a rate of $r\%$ compounded annually, and is repaid monthly for n years, then the regular monthly repayments, M, are given by

$$M = \frac{A(1 + r/100)^n(r/100)}{12((1 + r/100)^n - 1)}.$$

Chapter summary – pulling it all together

By the end of this chapter you should be able to:

	Confident ✓	Not confident?
Use scale factors to calculate percentage changes		Revise pages 28–29
Adjust nominal data to take inflation into account		Revise pages 29–30

	Confident ✓	Not confident?
Calculate index numbers for a time series		Revise pages 30–31
Work out future and present values of a single investment		Revise pages 32–35
Calculate total investment for a series of regular payments		Revise pages 35–37
Calculate the present value of an annuity		Revise pages 37–38
Calculate the monthly repayments of a loan		Revise pages 38–39

Now try the assessment question at the start of the chapter using the answer guidelines below.

Answer guidelines

✳ Assessment question

(a) Country A has twice the GDP of country B. In the future, the annual growth rates of these two countries are expected to be 2% and 6%, respectively. After how many years will the GDP of country B exceed that of country A?

(b) The sum of £4,000 is borrowed from a bank at a rate of 4.8% interest, compounded monthly. The loan is repaid in monthly instalments of £x. Find an expression, in terms of x, for the outstanding debt at the end of n months.

   (i)   How many months would it take to repay the loan if $x = £100$?

   (ii) What should the monthly repayment be if the debt is to be cleared after 18 months?

  (iii) Describe briefly what happens to the debt when $x = £16$.

Approaching the question

- Parts (a) and (b) of this question are unrelated.
- The answer to part (a) is independent of the actual values of GDP, which is why they are unspecified.
- The calculations in part (b) are similar to the worked example on page 38. However, there are differences, so you cannot simply use the formula given at the end of the worked example. You need to work from first principles, or adapt the given formula, to allow for the fact that interest is compounded monthly.
- Once the general result has been established, parts (i), (ii) and (iii) can be tackled by substituting values for x or n, and, in the case of (i) and (ii), solving an equation.

Method of solution

- For part (a), begin by denoting the current levels of GDP of the two countries by $2P$ and P, respectively, and write down expressions for these levels after n years, assuming growth rates of 2% and 6%. You can then equate the two expressions and use logs to solve the equation for n.
- The derivation of the general formula for part (a) follows the same logic as that of the worked example on debt repayment. If the annual interest rate is 4.8%, then the monthly rate is 0.4%. Each month the outstanding debt gets multiplied by 1.004, and x is subtracted for the repayment. Write down expressions for the debt at the end of the first, second, third months and so on, until a pattern can be spotted. You can then write down a lengthy expression for the debt after n months, and use the formula for the sum of a geometric series to write this down in a compact form.
  - For (i) put $x = 100$, equate the expression to zero and solve for n. You will need to use logs for this.
  - For (ii) put $n = 18$, equate the expression to zero, and solve for x.
  - For (iii) put $x = 16$ into the expression and comment on what happens.

Companion website

Go to the companion website at **www.pearsoned.co.uk/econexpress** to find more revision support online for this topic area.

Notes

3 Functions of one variable

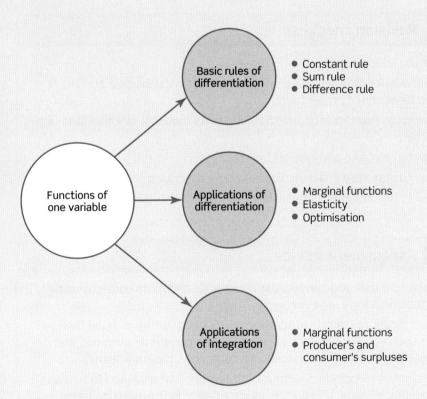

- Basic rules of differentiation
  - Constant rule
  - Sum rule
  - Difference rule

- Functions of one variable

- Applications of differentiation
  - Marginal functions
  - Elasticity
  - Optimisation

- Applications of integration
  - Marginal functions
  - Producer's and consumer's surpluses

A printable version of this topic map is available from **www.pearsoned.co.uk/econexpress**

Introduction

In this chapter we consider the calculus of functions of one variable. Economic variables are changing continually, and differentiation provides us with a technique for measuring their rate of change. We begin by describing the rules that enable us to differentiate any linear combination of power functions. There are many direct applications including the derivation of marginal functions, and the calculation of price elasticity of supply and demand. Differentiation can also be used to find the maximum and minimum values of a function. In particular, we can identify the quantity needed for a firm to maximise profit and minimise average costs.

The reverse of differentiation is integration, which enables us to go backwards and recover the original economic function, given its marginal function. Integration can also be used to calculate the area under a graph, and so we can use it to evaluate producer's and consumer's surpluses.

 Revision checklist

What you need to know:

❑ methods for differentiating and integrating functions that are simple combinations of power functions;

❑ how to go from an economic function to its marginal function (and vice versa);

❑ how to calculate and interpret elasticity;

❑ how to maximise and minimise economic functions;

❑ how to use integration to evaluate producer's and consumer's surpluses.

✳ **Assessment advice**

● Make sure that you can express reciprocals and roots correctly using indices (this topic was covered in Chapter 1).

● Don't forget to classify stationary points once you have found them; if the second-order derivative is negative the point is a maximum, and if it is positive it is a minimum (counter-intuitive as this may seem!)

● Remember to include constants of integration when asked to find an indefinite integral. Use additional information in the question to pin down its value.

● After integrating check (mentally, if not on paper) that your answer is correct by differentiating it to make sure that you get back to the original function.

Assessment question

Could you answer this question? Guidelines on answering the question are presented at the end of this chapter.

A firm's demand function for a particular good is given by $P = 200 - 2Q$.

Fixed costs are 200 and total variable costs are $Q^3 - 35Q^2 + 320Q$.

Find the level of output that maximises profit.

At this level of demand, evaluate

(a) price elasticity of demand;

(b) consumer's surplus.

Give an economic interpretation of each of your answers to parts (a) and (b).

Basic rules of differentiation

The line in Figure 3.1(a) passes through the points with coordinates (1,6) and (3,2). The gradient of this line can be worked out as the change in y divided by the change in x. If these changes are denoted by Δy and Δx, respectively, then

$$\text{Gradient} = \frac{\Delta y}{\Delta x} = \frac{2 - 6}{3 - 1} = \frac{-4}{2} = -2.$$

The fact that this is negative indicates that the line slopes downhill. The other cases of horizontal and uphill lines (shown in Figures 3.1b and 3.1c) have a zero and positive gradient, respectively.

For a curve, the gradient changes as we move along it. Figure 3.2 shows the graph of a function, $y = f(x)$, which gets steeper as x increases. The gradient at any point, $x = a$, on the graph is taken to be that of the tangent at a, is denoted by $f'(a)$, and is called the *derivative* of f at $x = a$.

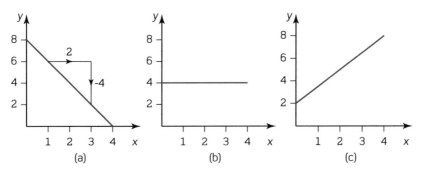

Figure 3.1

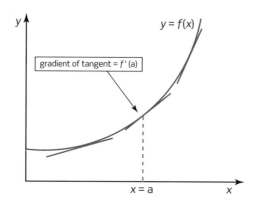

Figure 3.2

Fortunately, there is a simple way of working out the gradient without having to draw the curve:

if $f(x) = x^n$ then $f'(x) = nx^{n-1}$

(the power comes down to the front and one is subtracted from the power).

The expression $f'(x)$ is called the *derived function*, and the process of going from $f(x)$ to $f'(x)$ is called *differentiation*.

Using this power function rule: if $f(x) = x^{100}$ then $f'(x) = 100x^{99}$ and if $g(x) = x^{-4}$ then $g'(x) = -4x^{-5}$.

If the original function is given in the form $y = ...$, then the notation dy/dx is used as an alternative to $f'(x)$.

The constant, sum and difference rules enable us to differentiate simple combinations of power functions.

The constant rule: if $h(x) = cf(x)$ then $h'(x) = cf'(x)$.

This shows that if $y = 4x^7$ then

$$\frac{dy}{dx} = 4(7x^6) = 28x^6.$$

The sum rule: if $h(x) = f(x) + g(x)$ then $h'(x) = f'(x) + g'(x)$.

This shows that if $y = x^4 + x$ then

$$\frac{dy}{dx} = 4x^3 + 1$$

The difference rule: if $h(x) = f(x) - g(x)$ then $h'(x) = f'(x) - g'(x)$.

This shows that if $x^{-2} - x^{\frac{1}{2}}$ then

$$\frac{dy}{dx} = -2x^{-3} - \frac{1}{2}x^{\frac{1}{2}}.$$

It is possible to put all three rules together and differentiate an expression term-by-term.

Worked example

If

$$f(x) = \frac{6}{x} + 3x^2 + 4,$$

evaluate the first- and second-order derivatives, $f'(1)$ and $f''(1)$.

Give a graphical interpretation of these results.

Solution

In order to differentiate an expression like this we must first write each term in index notation (see Chapter 1). In this case we have $f(x) = 6x^{-1} + 3x^2 + 4$, so

$$f'(x) = 6(-1x^{-2}) + 3(2x) = -6x^{-2} + 6x = -\frac{6}{x^2} + 6x.$$

Notice that the constant term 4 differentiates to zero. This is because the graph of $y = 4$ is horizontal (see Figure 3.1b) so has zero gradient at all points.

The second-order derivative $f''(x)$ (sometimes written $\frac{d^2y}{dx^2}$) is found by differentiating a second time to get

$$f''(x) = -6(-2x^{-3}) + 6 = 12x^{-3} + 6 = \frac{12}{x^3} + 6.$$

Substituting $x = 1$ into both of the above expressions gives $f'(1) = 0$ and $f''(1) = 18$.

The fact that $f'(1) = 0$ shows that the tangent to the graph of $f(x)$ is horizontal at $x = 1$.

The fact that $f''(1) > 0$ shows that the gradient itself is increasing so the graph bends upwards (i.e. concave from above). These features are illustrated in Figure 3.3.

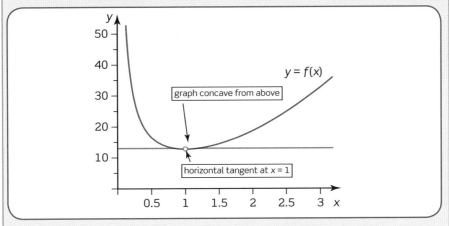

Figure 3.3

Test yourself

Q1. Find the derivative of each of the following functions at the specified point:

(a) $y = 5x^2 - 2x + 4$ at $x = 3$;

(b) $y = 2\sqrt{x} - 3x^4$ at $x = 1$;

(c) $y = \dfrac{1}{x^2} - \dfrac{1}{x} - 10$ at $x = 2$.

In each case, state whether the gradient of the graph of the function is uphill, downhill or horizontal at that point.

Applications of differentiation

Key definitions

Marginal revenue is the derivative of total revenue:

$$MR = \frac{d(TR)}{dQ}.$$

Marginal cost is the derivative of total cost:

$$MC = \frac{d(TC)}{dQ}.$$

Marginal propensity to consume is the derivative of consumption:

$$MPC = \frac{dC}{dY}.$$

Marginal propensity to save is the derivative of savings:

$$MPS = \frac{dS}{dY}.$$

Marginal product of labour is the derivative of output:

$$MP_L = \frac{dQ}{dL}.$$

You may be familiar with alternative definitions of marginal functions. For example, marginal revenue is sometimes given as the change in revenue brought about by a one-unit increase in quantity. Figure 3.4 shows that this version gives the gradient of the chord on the total revenue curve. Although this is not the same as that of the tangent, it gives a fairly good approximation.

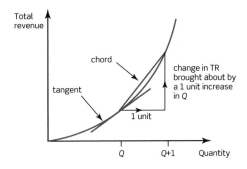

Figure 3.4

Worked example

A firm's average cost function is given by

$$AC = Q + 8 + \frac{400}{Q}.$$

Find the marginal cost when $Q = 12$, and hence estimate the increase in total cost when supply increases by 0.5 units.

Solution

We are given the average cost function so we first multiply by Q to find the total cost:

$$TC = \left(Q + 8 + \frac{400}{Q}\right)Q = Q^2 + 8Q + 400.$$

We now differentiate this to find the marginal cost:

$$MC = \frac{d(TC)}{dQ} = 2Q + 8.$$

Substituting $Q = 12$ into this formula gives $MC = 32$.

This is the approximate change in TC when Q increases by one unit so an estimate for the change in TC due to a 0.5-unit increase in Q is
$\Delta(TC) \approx 32 \times 0.5 = 16.$

Test yourself

Q2. If the demand function of a good is $P + 2Q = 400$, find an expression for the marginal revenue function. Find the value of MR when $Q = 24$ and hence estimate the change in TR brought about by a two-unit increase in Q at this point.

Q3. Find the marginal propensity to consume at $Y = 100$ when the consumption function is $C = 100 + 4\sqrt{Y}$. Hence, or otherwise, find the marginal propensity to save at this point.

Q4. A firm's short-run production function is $Q = 3L^2 - 0.1L^3$. Find the value of the marginal product of labour for $L = 5, 10, 15, 20$ and 25. Comment on your results.

Key definition

Price elasticity of supply (or demand) is given by:

$$\frac{\text{percentage change in quantity}}{\text{percentage change in price}}$$

This measures the responsiveness of supply (or demand) to changes in price. For example, if the price elasticity of supply is 2, then the percentage change in the quantity supplied is double that of the percentage price change. Suppliers would respond to a 5% increase in price by increasing the quantity they supply to the market by 10%.

If the supply or demand functions are known, then differentiation can be used to work out the value of E using the formula

$$E = \frac{P}{Q} \times \frac{dQ}{dP}$$

Worked example

Find the price elasticity of supply at $P = 10$ for a good with supply function $Q = -0.05P^2 + 3P - 5$.

Solution

$$\frac{dQ}{dP} = -0.1P + 3.$$

Substituting $P = 10$ into the above expressions for Q and

$$\frac{dQ}{dP}$$

give $Q = -0.05 \times 10^2 + 3 \times 10 - 5 = 20$ and

$$\frac{dQ}{dP} = -0.1 \times 10 + 3 = 2.$$

Hence

$$E = \frac{P}{Q} \times \frac{dQ}{dP} = \frac{10}{20} \times 2 = 1.$$

It follows that the percentage changes in price and supply are exactly equal at this price. We describe this by saying that supply is *unit-elastic* at $P = 10$.

The words *elastic* and *inelastic* are used to describe the responsiveness of supply when $E > 1$ and $E < 1$, respectively.

Test yourself

Q5. Find a general expression for the price elasticity of demand, in terms of P, for the demand function $Q = 120 - 2P$.

(a) For what price is demand unit elastic?

(b) Find the elasticity when $P = 10$ and hence estimate the change in demand when prices decrease by 4%.

Key definition

A function has a **stationary point** at $x = a$ if $f'(a) = 0$. In addition, if $f''(a) > 0$, the point is a minimum; if $f''(a) < 0$, it is a maximum.

These points are illustrated in Figure 3.5 which shows that at both points the tangent is horizontal. At the minimum point, the graph bends upwards (concave from above) and at the maximum point the graph bends downwards (convex from above).

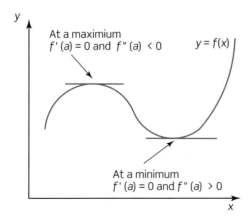

Figure 3.5

Worked example

In a competitive market, the supply and demand functions of a good are given by $P = 2Q_S + 15$ and $P = -2Q_D + 95$.

The government imposes a tax of t per unit sold. Assuming that equilibrium conditions prevail in the market, and that the producers adjust the supply function to include the tax, find the value of t that maximises tax revenue. What is the effect of this tax on the equilibrium market price?

Solution

After the imposition of the tax, the new supply equation is obtained by replacing P with $P - t$ because the producers receive the price that the consumer pays, less the tax that is passed on to the government:
$P - t = 2Q_S + 15$ or equivalently $P = 2Q_S + 15 + t$.

In equilibrium $Q_S = Q_D = Q$, so the supply and demand equations become $P = 2Q + 15 + t$ and $P = -2Q + 95$, respectively.

Hence $2Q + 15 + t = -2Q + 95$ (since both sides are equal to P);

$$Q = 20 - \frac{t}{4} \text{ (solving for } Q\text{)}.$$

This can be substituted into either the supply or demand equation to find the equilibrium price. The demand equation gives:

$$P = -2Q + 95 = -2\left(20 - \frac{t}{4}\right) + 95 = \frac{t}{2} + 55 \qquad (3.1)$$

The government receives t per unit so, if Q units are sold, the total tax revenue is given by:

$$T = tQ = t\left(20 - \frac{t}{4}\right) = 20t - \frac{t^2}{4}.$$

This is the expression to be maximised.

The stationary point can be found by differentiating once and equating to zero:

$$\frac{dT}{dt} = 20 - \frac{t}{2} = 0,$$

which has solution $t = 40$.

To classify the point we differentiate a second time:

$$\frac{d^2T}{dt^2} = -\frac{1}{2},$$

which is negative, confirming that the stationary point is a maximum.

To compare the pre- and post-tax equilibrium prices, all we need to do is to substitute $t = 0$ and $t = 40$ into Equation 3.1.

Before tax, the price is 55 and after tax this increases to 75. Therefore, the consumer pays an additional 20 units and the remaining 20 units must be paid by the firm.

Test yourself

Q6. The demand function of a good is given by $P = a - bQ$, where a and b are positive constants. Find the value of Q that maximises total revenue.

Applications of integration

Integration reverses the effect of differentiation and takes you back to the original function.

We know, for example, that the function $2x^5 - 4x$ differentiates to $10x^4 - 4$ so we say that $2x^5 - 4x$ is the integral of $10x^4 - 4$. Also, because constants differentiate to zero, the same is true of $2x^5 - 4x + c$ for any constant, c (called the *constant of integration*).

We write $\int 10x^4 - 4 \, dx = 2x^5 - 4x + c.$

In general, we have

$$\int x^n \, dx = \frac{1}{n+1}x^{n+1} + c. \text{ (Check that } \frac{x^{n+1}}{n+1} + c \text{ differentiates to } x^n.\text{)}$$

This works for all values of $n \neq -1$. The case when $n = -1$ is dealt with in Chapter 4.

To integrate a power function you first add one to the power and then divide by the number you get; because integration is just the reverse of differentiation, we can integrate term-by-term:

$$\int 7x^4 - 6x^2 + 3x \, dx = 7\left(\frac{x^5}{5}\right) - 6\left(\frac{x^3}{3}\right) + 3\left(\frac{x^2}{2}\right) + c$$

$$= \frac{7x^5}{5} - 2x^3 + \frac{3x^2}{2} + c.$$

Starting with any economic function, we differentiate to obtain the corresponding marginal function. Integration allows us to go the other way, so we can find the original economic function from the marginal function.

If a firm's fixed costs are 13 and the marginal cost function is given by $MC = 4Q + 5$, we can integrate to find the total cost function,

$$TC = \int 4Q + 5 \, dQ = 4\left(\frac{Q^2}{2}\right) + 5Q + c = 2Q^2 + 5Q + c.$$

The constant of integration term, c, is independent of output so must represent the fixed costs, which are 13 in this case.

Hence $TC = 2Q^2 + 5Q + 13$.

If the marginal propensity to consume is given by

$$MPC = 0.3 + \frac{0.5}{\sqrt{Y}} = 0.3 + 0.5Y^{-1/2},$$

we can integrate to find the consumption function:

$$C = \int 0.3 + 0.5Y^{-1/2} dY = 0.3Y + 0.5\left(\frac{Y^{1/2}}{1/2}\right) + c = 0.3Y + \sqrt{Y} + c.$$

The constant of integration can be assigned a specific value if we have some extra information. For example, if consumption is 14 when $Y = 25$ then we substitute this into the consumption function $0.3 \times 25 + \sqrt{25} + c = 14$, which gives $c = 1.5$. Hence $C = 0.3Y + \sqrt{Y} + 1.5$.

Integration can also be used to find the exact area under the graph of a function. The area under the square function shown in Figure 3.6 between $x = 2$ and $x = 5$ is written as $\int_2^5 x^2 \, dx$ (the numbers 2 and 5 are called *limits of integration*).

It is evaluated by first integrating x^2 to get $x^3/3$. We then substitute the limits 5 and 2 into this and subtract:

$$\int_2^5 x^2 \, dx = \left[\frac{x^3}{3}\right]_2^5 = \frac{5^3}{3} - \frac{2^3}{3} = \frac{125}{3} - \frac{8}{3} = \frac{117}{3}.$$

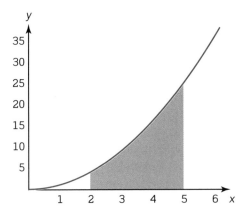

Figure 3.6

Key definitions

Consumer's surplus (CS): excess cost that the consumer would have been prepared to pay for goods over and above what was actually paid.

Producer's surplus (PS): excess revenue that a producer has actually received over and above the lower revenue that it was prepared to accept for the supply of its goods.

If (Q_0, P_0) lies on a demand curve $P = f(Q)$ and (Q_0, P_0) also lies on a supply curve $P = g(Q)$,

$$CS = \int_0^{Q_0} f(Q)\, dQ - Q_0 P_0$$

$$PS = Q_0 P_0 - \int_0^{Q_0} g(Q)\, dQ.$$

Worked example

If the demand function of a good is $P = 300 - 2Q^2$ and the market price is 100, calculate the consumer's surplus.

Solution

The demand when $P = 100$ satisfies the equation $300 - 2Q^2 = 100$, which is easily solved to get $Q = 10$.

The demand function sketched in Figure 3.7 shows the different prices that consumers are prepared to pay for various quantities of the good. The area of the rectangle, OABC, is $10 \times 100 = 1000$ and gives the cost of buying 10 units of the good priced at 100 each. However, as the graph shows, consumers would actually have been prepared to pay the higher price indicated by the demand curve for quantities up to the 10th item. Therefore, the shaded area represents the benefit to the consumers of paying the fixed price of 100 for all items. The consumer's surplus is therefore given by Area BCD = Area OABD − Area OABC

$$= \int_0^{10} 300 - 2Q^2 \, dQ - 1000$$

$$= \left[300Q - \frac{2Q^3}{3} \right]_0^{10} - 1000$$

$$= \left(300 \times 10 - \frac{2 \times 10^3}{3} \right) - (0) - 1000$$

$$= \frac{4000}{3}.$$

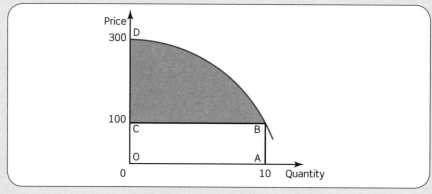

Figure 3.7

Test yourself

Q7. If the marginal revenue of a good is $MR = 200 - 6Q^2$, find the total revenue function and deduce the corresponding demand function.

Q8. Given the demand function $P = 28 - Q_D^2$ and the supply function $P = 2Q_S + 4$, find the producer's and consumer's surpluses, assuming pure competition.

Chapter summary – pulling it all together

By the end of this chapter you should be able to:

	Confident? ✓	Not confident?
Differentiate simple combinations of power functions		Revise pages 45–48
Find marginal functions in economics		Revise pages 48–50
Evaluate price elasticity of supply and demand		Revise pages 50–51
Find the maximum and minimum points of economic functions		Revise pages 51–53
Integrate marginal functions		Revise pages 53–54
Evaluate consumer's and producer's surpluses		Revise pages 55–56

Now try the assessment question at the start of the chapter using the answer guidelines below.

Answer guidelines

✳ Assessment question

A firm's demand function for a particular good is given by $P = 200 - 2Q$.

Fixed costs are 200 and total variable costs are $Q^3 - 35Q^2 + 320Q$.

Find the level of output that maximises profit.

At this level of demand, evaluate:

(a) price elasticity of demand;

(b) consumer's surplus.

Give an economic interpretation of each of your answers to parts (a) and (b).

Approaching the question

- This question is in four parts. You need the answer to the first part in order to complete the rest of the question.
- Decide at the beginning exactly what individual steps are needed to tackle each part.
- Although there are no watertight checks you can do to guarantee that you have made no mistakes, you should at least make sure that your answers seem sensible before moving on to the next part.

Method of solution

- Profit $\pi = TR - TC$, so the first thing that you need to do is to write down expressions for TR and TC.
  - Total revenue is PQ so you just multiply the given demand function by Q.
  - Total cost is the sum of the variable costs and fixed costs, both of which are given.
  - Be careful when subtracting TC from TR. The whole of TC must be taken away. It helps if you put brackets round TC to begin with.

- To find the stationary points you differentiate and equate to zero.
  - This gives a quadratic that can be solved either by factorisation or by using the formula (see Chapter 1 if you need to revise this).
  - The quadratic has two solutions. The best way to classify them is to use the second derivative, although other approaches are possible. You should expect one of the stationary points to be a maximum and the other to be a minimum.

- Part (a) asks you to calculate the price elasticity of demand.
  - This can be done using the formula given in this chapter. Note that it requires

    $$\frac{dQ}{dP}.$$

    This can be found either by rearranging the demand equation to make Q the subject or by finding

    $$\frac{dP}{dQ}$$

and using the result,

$$\frac{dQ}{dP} = 1 \div \frac{dP}{dQ}$$

(which is explained in Chapter 4).

- Demand elasticity is negative because the demand curve slopes downhill. To avoid this, some economists put a minus sign in front of the definition given in this chapter to make the answer positive. Make sure that you follow the convention adopted by your own lecturer.

- Part (b) asks you to calculate the consumer's surplus. This can be done using the formula on page 55.

- The last part asks you to interpret your results. To gain full marks here it is important that you explain what these results mean in *economic* terms, referencing the particular numbers that you have found in parts (a) and (b). You have already shown the examiner that you have the skills needed to perform the calculation so there is no need to repeat this. This is your opportunity to show that you know what the terms "price elasticity of demand" and "consumer's surplus" actually mean.

Companion website

Go to the companion website at **www.pearsoned.co.uk/econexpress** to find more revision support online for this topic area.

Notes

Further differentiation and integration

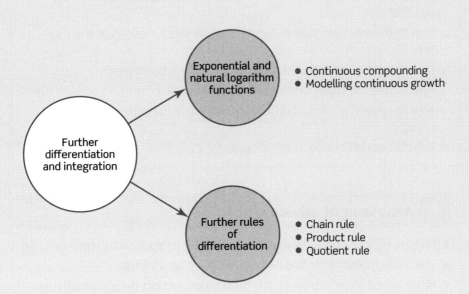

Exponential and natural logarithm functions
- Continuous compounding
- Modelling continuous growth

Further differentiation and integration

Further rules of differentiation
- Chain rule
- Product rule
- Quotient rule

A printable version of this topic map is available from **www.pearsoned.co.uk/econexpress**

Introduction

The three rules described in Chapter 3 are used to differentiate linear combinations of functions such as quadratics. In this chapter we introduce the chain, product and quotient rules, which allow us to differentiate more complicated functions such as $x\sqrt{(2x-3)}$. These new rules also provide us with a means of establishing several important theoretical relationships between economic variables. Two new functions are considered: the exponential and natural logarithm functions, e^x and $\ln(x)$. These functions are used widely to model continuous growth and decay.

 Revision checklist

What you need to know:
- ❏ the formula for continuous compounding;
- ❏ how to model continuous growth and decay using exponential functions;
- ❏ how to differentiate and integrate exponential functions of the form e^{mx};
- ❏ how to differentiate the natural logarithm function $\ln(mx)$;
- ❏ how to use the chain, product and quotient rules;
- ❏ how to apply the rules of differentiation to derive general economic results;
- ❏ the connection between dQ/dP and dP/dQ.

✳ Assessment advice

- Make sure that you can evaluate e^x and $\ln(x)$ on your calculator.
- Learn the formulae for the derivatives of e^{mx} and $\ln(mx)$.
- When asked to differentiate any particular function, decide which rules are needed before you begin.
- Try to remember the rules informally (e.g. the chain rule could be remembered as "differentiate the outer function and then multiply by the derivative of the inner function").
- When finding elasticity, check that you are given an expression for Q in terms of P. If not, consider using the result $dQ/dP = 1 \div dP/dQ$ to avoid having to rearrange the demand or supply functions.

Assessment question

Could you answer this question? Guidelines on answering the question are presented at the end of this chapter.

(a) By applying the product rule to $TR = PQ$, show that marginal revenue can be expressed as

$$MR = P\left(1 + \frac{1}{E}\right),$$

where E is the price elasticity of demand.

(b) Use the result from part (a) to show that when demand is elastic, total revenue rises as the price decreases.

(c) Given the demand equation, $Q = 100e^{-0.1P}$, find the elasticity when $P = 10$. Use the formula from part (a) to deduce the value of MR at this point and give an interpretation of this result.

Exponential and natural logarithm functions

We saw in Chapter 2 that when a principal, P, is invested at an annual rate of $r\%$, which is compounded k times a year, the future value after t years is given by

$$S = P\left(1 + \frac{r}{100k}\right)^{kt}.$$

Table 4.1 shows the future values when £500 is invested for a year at 4% interest, when compounding occurs annually, semi-annually, monthly, weekly and daily. As expected, the return rises as the frequency of compounding increases. What you might not have expected, however, is that the numbers in Table 4.1 appear to be approaching a particular value or limit. This situation, in which the investment is compounded with ever-increasing frequency, is described as *continuous compounding*, and the future value can be worked out using the formula

$$S = Pe^{\frac{rt}{100}}$$

where

$$e = \lim_{n \to \infty}\left(1 + \frac{1}{n}\right)^n = 2.71828182\ldots$$

Table 4.1

Annually	Semi-annually	Monthly	Weekly	Daily
£520	£520.20	£520.37	£520.40	£520.40

The number e is a special constant in mathematics (rather like the number π) and has many important properties.

Key definition

Logarithms to base e are called **natural logarithms** and ln(x) is used as an alternative to $\log_e x$.

Worked example

A principal of £25,000 is invested at 6% interest compounded continuously.

(a) Find its future value after 3 years.
(b) How long will it take for the value of an investment to double?

Solution

In this case $r = 6$, so after t years the future value is $S = Pe^{0.06t}$.

(a) Setting $t = 3$ and $P = 25{,}000$ gives $S = 25000e^{0.18} = £29930.43$.
(b) An investment doubles when $S = 2P$, so the time taken satisfies $Pe^{0.06t} = 2P$.

The Ps cancel so t is the solution of the equation $e^{0.06t} = 2$. Taking natural logs gives $0.06t = \ln 2$ so $t = 11.55$. The answer is given in years, so the investment is doubled after 11 years and 201 days.

Test yourself

Q1. A principal of £1,000 is invested at 7% interest compounded continuously.

(a) Find its future value after 4 years.
(b) Find the AER (annual equivalent rate).

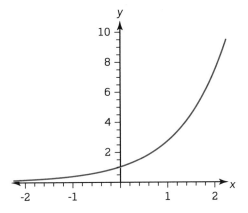

Figure 4.1

Functions such as 2^x, 3^x and 10^x are all referred to as exponential functions. The graphs of these functions all have the same basic shape, shown in Figure 4.1, and they all pass through (0, 1).

In the case when the base is e, the function is called THE exponential function, and it has the remarkable property that it differentiates to itself, so that the gradient at each point on the graph of Figure 4.1 is the same as the function value at that point.

Quite generally we have:

$$\frac{d(e^{mx})}{dx} = me^{mx}$$

and

$$\frac{d(\ln(mx))}{dx} = \frac{1}{x}.$$

so that e^{-5x} differentiates to $-5e^{-5x}$ and $\ln(7x)$ differentiates to $\frac{1}{x}$.

Worked example

During a recession, monthly sales, Y, of a good (modelled as a continuous variable) decrease exponentially so that t months after the beginning of the recession, sales are given by $Y = 2500\,e^{-0.02t}$.

(a) State the monthly sales at the start of the recession.

(b) Find the rate of decrease of sales after 6 months.

(c) The firm decides that it cannot afford to maintain production when monthly sales are fewer than 1,200. After how many months does this happen?

Solution

(a) Setting $t = 0$ into the previous formula gives $Y = 2500$ because $e^0 = 1$.

(b) The rate of change is given by

$$\frac{dY}{dt} = -50\, e^{-0.02t}$$

because

$$\frac{d(e^{-0.02t})}{dt} = -0.02e^{-0.02t}.$$

At $t = 6$,

$$\frac{dY}{dt} = -50 \times e^{-0.12} = -44$$

so sales are decreasing at a rate of about 44 per month.

(c) The equation $2500e^{-0.02t} = 1200$ can be solved by dividing both sides by 2,500 and then taking logs:

$$e^{-0.02t} = 0.48$$
$$-0.02t = \ln(0.48)$$
$$t = 36.7$$

Production ceases during the 37th month after the start of the recession.

Test yourself

Q2. A financial advisor predicts that an investment will double in value every 8 years. A principal of £500 is invested. The future value after t years is denoted by S.

(a) If $S = Ae^{mt}$, find the values of A and m.

(b) Find the rate at which the investment is increasing when $t = 20$.

The results for the differentiation of the functions e^{mx} and $\ln(mx)$ given on page 65 can be recast in the form of two important integrals:

$$\int e^{mx}\,dx = \frac{1}{m}e^{mx} + c$$

and

$$\int \frac{1}{x}\,dx = \ln(x) + c$$

for any constant of integration, c.

In Chapter 3, we noted the result

$$\int x^n\,dx = \frac{1}{n+1}x^{n+1} + c$$

provided that $n \neq -1$. (This exception is not allowed because we cannot divide by 0.) The above result for the integration of $1/x$ fills the gap, showing that the reciprocal function, $1/x$, integrates to the natural logarithm function. For example,

$$\int_1^3 \frac{2}{x}\,dx = [2\ln x]_1^3 = 2\ln 3 - 2\ln 1 = 2\ln 3 = 2.20.$$

In Chapter 2 we discussed the idea of an annuity, which is a fund designed to provide a series of regular future payments. The present value of an annuity is the lump sum that needs to be invested now in order to secure these payments for the desired number of years. If this fund is to provide a continuous revenue stream for n years, at an annual rate of S pounds per year, then the present value is worked out by evaluating the definite integral:

$$P = \int_0^n S e^{-rt/100}\,dt$$

Worked example

Calculate the present value of a continuous revenue stream for 8 years, at a constant rate of £900 a year, if the discount rate is 4.8%.

Solution

Putting $S = 900$, $r = 4.8$ and $n = 8$ into the above formula gives

$$P = \int_0^8 900 e^{-0.048t}\,dt = \left[\frac{900}{-0.048}e^{-0.048t}\right]_0^8$$

$$= -18750(e^{-0.384} - e^0) = £5978.79$$

Q3. Calculate the present value of a continuous revenue stream for 5 years, at a constant rate of £2,000 a year, if the discount rate is 5%.

Further rules of differentiation

Key definition

The **chain rule** states that if y is a function of u, which is itself a function of x, then

$$\frac{dy}{dx} = \frac{dy}{du} \times \frac{du}{dx}$$

The chain rule shows how to differentiate a function of a function (known as a composite function): differentiate the outer function and multiply by the derivative of the inner function.

The formal approach to differentiating the function $y = (3x^2 + 4)^7$ is to let $u = 3x^2 + 4$ so that $y = u^7$.

Hence

$$\frac{dy}{du} = 7u^6 = 7(3x^2 + 4)^6.$$

and

$$\frac{du}{dx} = 6x.$$

The chain rule gives

$$\frac{dy}{dx} = \frac{dy}{du} \times \frac{du}{dx} = 7(3x^2 + 4)^6 \times 6x = 42x(3x^2 + 4)^6.$$

With practice, the logic can be done in your head and the answer written down without working. For example, to differentiate $y = (x^2 + 3x - 9)^4$, you first differentiate the outer power function to get $4(x^2 + 3x - 9)^3$, and then multiply by the derivative of the inner function, $x^2 + 3x + 9$, which is $2x + 3$, so

$$\frac{dy}{dx} = 4(x^2 + 3x - 9)^3 (2x + 3).$$

Key definition

The **product rule** states that if $y = uv$, where u and v are both functions of x, then

$$\frac{dy}{dx} = u\frac{dv}{dx} + v\frac{du}{dx}$$

The product rule shows how to differentiate the product of two functions: multiply each function by the derivative of the other and add.

To differentiate $y = x^2e^{3x}$, we write $u = x^2$ and $v = e^{3x}$ so that

$$\frac{du}{dx} = 2x$$

and

$$\frac{dv}{dx} = 3e^{3x}.$$

The product rule then gives

$$\frac{dy}{dx} = u\frac{dv}{dx} + v\frac{du}{dx}$$
$$= x^2 \times 3e^{3x} + e^{3x} \times 2x$$
$$= x(3x + 2)e^{3x}.$$

Key definition

The **quotient rule** states that if

$$y = \frac{u}{v}$$

where u and v are both functions of x, then

$$\frac{dy}{dx} = \frac{v\dfrac{du}{dx} - u\dfrac{dv}{dx}}{v^2}$$

The quotient rule shows how to differentiate the quotient of two functions: bottom times derivative of top, minus top times derivative of bottom, all over bottom squared.

To differentiate

$$y = \frac{2x - 1}{3x + 1},$$

we write $u = 2x - 1$ and $v = 3x + 1$ so that

$$\frac{du}{dx} = 2$$

and

$$\frac{dv}{dx} = 3.$$

The quotient rule then gives

$$\frac{dy}{dx} = \frac{v\dfrac{du}{dx} - u\dfrac{dv}{dx}}{v^2}$$

$$= \frac{(3x + 1)(2) - (2x - 1)(3)}{(3x + 1)^2}$$

$$= \frac{6x + 2 - 6x + 3}{(3x + 1)^2}$$

$$= \frac{5}{(3x + 1)^2}$$

Test yourself

Q4. Differentiate:

(a) $\ln(x^2 + 4)$

(b) $x\sqrt{2x + 1}$

(c) $\dfrac{x}{3x + 4}$

Worked example

A firm's demand function is given by $P = \sqrt{100 - 2Q}$.

(a) Find expressions for total revenue and marginal revenue.

(b) Find the value of Q that maximises total revenue.

Solution

(a) $TR = PQ = Q\sqrt{100 - 2Q}$.

An expression for marginal revenue can be obtained by differentiating TR using the product rule. If we write

$$u = Q; v = (100 - 2Q)^{\frac{1}{2}}$$

then

$$\frac{du}{dQ} = 1; \frac{dv}{dQ} = \frac{1}{2}(100 - 2Q)^{-\frac{1}{2}}(-2) = \frac{-1}{\sqrt{100 - 2Q}} \text{ (chain rule)}.$$

The product rule gives

$$MR = -\frac{Q}{\sqrt{100 - 2Q}} + 1 \times \sqrt{100 - 2Q}$$

$$= \frac{-Q + (100 - 2Q)}{\sqrt{100 - 2Q}}$$

$$= \frac{100 - 3Q}{\sqrt{100 - 2Q}}$$

(b) Total revenue is maximised when

$$\frac{d(TR)}{dQ} = 0.$$

From part (a) this occurs when $100 - 3Q = 0$, so $Q = 100 / 3$.

To classify this stationary point we differentiate a second time by using the quotient rule to find an expression for the derivative of MR. If we write $u = 100 - 3Q; v = (100 - 2Q)^{\frac{1}{2}}$, then

$$\frac{du}{dQ} = -3; \frac{dv}{dQ} = \frac{-1}{\sqrt{100 - 2Q}}$$

where the chain rule has been used to differentiate v, as before.

The quotient rule gives

$$\frac{d^2(TR)}{dQ^2} = \frac{\sqrt{100 - 2Q} \times (-3) - (100 - 3Q) \times \frac{-1}{\sqrt{100 - 2Q}}}{100 - 2Q}$$

There is little to be gained by simplifying this expression because we are only interested in its sign when $Q = 100/3$. If this is substituted, then the second term in the numerator is zero and we are left with

$$\frac{-3\sqrt{\dfrac{100}{3}}}{\dfrac{100}{3}} = -\frac{3\sqrt{3}}{10}$$

This is negative, confirming that the stationary point is a maximum.

Test yourself

Q5. A firm's total cost function is $TC = 20\, e^{0.01Q}$. Find the value of Q that minimises the average cost, and verify that at this level of output $AC = MC$.

The result of this "Test yourself" question is true for all total cost functions and can be proved in general easily. Average cost is defined to be total cost divided by quantity so

$$AC = \frac{TC}{Q}.$$

If we put $u = TC$ and $v = Q$, then

$$\frac{du}{dQ} = \frac{d(TC)}{dQ} = MC$$

and

$$\frac{dQ}{dQ} = 1.$$

The quotient rule gives

$$\frac{d(AC)}{dQ} = \frac{Q \times MC - TC \times 1}{Q^2}.$$

At a stationary point,

$$\frac{d(AC)}{dQ} = 0$$

so $Q \times MC = TC$.

This can be rearranged as

$$MC = \frac{TC}{Q},$$

so $MC = AC$ at a stationary point. This shows that, when drawn on the same diagram, the graphs of MC and AC intersect at the stationary points of the AC curve.

Test yourself

Q6. (a) Use the quotient rule to show that if

$$\frac{d(AC)}{dQ} = \frac{Q \times MC - TC}{Q^2}$$

then

$$\frac{d^2(AC)}{dQ^2} = \frac{1}{Q}\frac{d(MC)}{dQ} - \frac{2}{Q^3}(Q \times MC - TC).$$

(b) Use the result of part (a) to show that at a stationary point on the AC curve,

$$\frac{d^2(AC)}{dQ^2} = \frac{1}{Q}\frac{d(MC)}{dQ}$$

and deduce that at a minimum point on the AC curve, the graph of MC is increasing.

In Chapter 3, elasticity of demand was defined to be

$$E = \frac{P}{Q} \times \frac{dQ}{dP}.$$

This formula assumes that Q is given in terms of P. Unfortunately this is not always the case. The demand function may well be given the other way round, with P written in terms of Q. It can be difficult (and sometimes impossible) to rearrange this to make Q the subject. The chain rule provides an alternative way of dealing with this. The formal statement of the chain rule is

$$\frac{dy}{dx} = \frac{dy}{du} \times \frac{du}{dx}$$

so that

$$\frac{dQ}{dQ} = \frac{dQ}{dP} \times \frac{dP}{dQ}.$$

Of course, $dQ/dQ = 1$. Hence

$$\frac{dQ}{dP} = \frac{1}{dP/dQ}$$

so an alternative formula for elasticity is

$$\boxed{E = \frac{P}{Q} \times \frac{1}{dP/dQ}}$$

Worked example

A firm's demand function is given by $P = 80 - Q^2$.

Find the elasticity of demand when $P = 55$, and state whether demand is elastic, inelastic or unit elastic at this price.

Solution

In this case P is given in terms of Q so we begin by finding the derivative,

$$\frac{dP}{dQ} = -2Q.$$

Hence

$$\frac{dQ}{dP} = \frac{1}{dP/dQ} = \frac{-1}{2Q},$$

giving

$$E = \frac{P}{Q} \times \frac{dQ}{dP} = \frac{P}{Q} \times \frac{1}{-2Q} = \frac{-P}{2Q^2} = \frac{-P}{2(80 - P)}.$$

Substituting $P = 55$ gives

$$E = \frac{-55}{2(80 - 55)} = -1.1.$$

The demand is elastic because $E < -1$ (or equivalently, since $|E| > 1$).

Test yourself

Q7. Find the elasticity at $Q = 15$ for the supply function $P = 20 + 3Q + 0.2Q^2$ and state whether supply is elastic, inelastic or unit elastic at this quantity.

Chapter summary – pulling it all together

By the end of this chapter you should be able to:

	Confident ✓	Not confident?
Solve problems involving continuous compounding		Revise pages 63–64
Work out the rates of change of exponential functions modelling continuous growth and decay		Revise pages 65–66
Integrate exponential functions		Revise pages 67–68
Use the chain, product and quotient rules		Revise pages 68–72
Use the three rules to derive general results in economics		Revise pages 72–73
Use the result $\dfrac{dQ}{dP} = \dfrac{1}{dP/dQ}$ when finding elasticity		Revise pages 73–74

Now try the assessment question at the start of the chapter using the answer guidelines below.

Answer guidelines

✳ Assessment question

(a) By applying the product rule to $TR = PQ$, show that marginal revenue can be expressed as

$$MR = P\left(1 + \frac{1}{E}\right),$$

where E is the price elasticity of demand.

(b) Use the result from part (a) to show that when demand is elastic, total revenue rises as the price decreases.

(c) Given the demand equation $Q = 100e^{-0.1P}$, find the elasticity when $P = 10$. Use the formula in part (a) to deduce the value of MR at this point and give an interpretation of this result.

Approaching the question

- This question is in three parts. It is structured so that if you cannot do the first part (which is the most difficult), you can still attempt the remaining parts. In fact, you can tackle this question in any order so you may prefer to do either (b) or (c) first.
- Part (a) is a standard result that you have seen before and probably copied down in your lecture notes. It is worthwhile learning the derivation of these theoretical results to give you more time in an exam to answer other questions that cannot be memorised in advance.
- Mathematical applications require you to do two things: perform a particular technique correctly and relate the result to the underlying economic concepts. In part (c) you need to calculate E using the standard formula, and then make a comment on the implications of this answer.

Method of solution

- The formal statement of the product rule is given on page 69. To tackle part (a) you need to work as follows:
  - The factors are P and Q, so you can write $u = P$ and $v = Q$ and then use the result $dQ/dQ = 1$.
  - To obtain the final expression in terms of E, write down the formula for E, rearrange to make dQ/dP the subject and then substitute this into the expression obtained from the product rule.

    The result $dQ/dP = 1 \div dP/dQ$ is helpful.

- The value of E is negative for a demand curve. If demand is elastic then $E < -1$. What does this tell you about the sign of MR and what in turn does this imply about the graph of TR? Remember that MR gives the gradient of the TR function when plotted against Q. In this question you need to think what happens to TR when the *price* decreases.
- For part (c) you need to use the result that the exponential function e^{mx} differentiates to me^{mx}, together with the formula for elasticity of demand given on page 73, to calculate the numerical value of E. This can be substituted into the result of part (a). It gives an interesting answer that can be interpreted fairly easily.

Companion website

Go to the companion website at **www.pearsoned.co.uk/econexpress** to find more revision support online for this topic area.

Notes

Notes

5 Functions of several variables

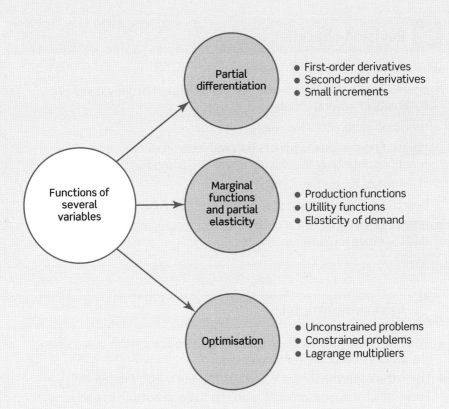

Functions of several variables

- Partial differentiation
  - First-order derivatives
  - Second-order derivatives
  - Small increments

- Marginal functions and partial elasticity
  - Production functions
  - Utillity functions
  - Elasticity of demand

- Optimisation
  - Unconstrained problems
  - Constrained problems
  - Lagrange multipliers

A printable version of this topic map is available from **www.pearsoned.co.uk/econexpress**

Introduction

Most relationships in economics involve more than just two variables. Demand for any particular good depends on the price of this good, the prices of substitutable and complimentary goods, advertising expenditure, consumers' tastes, and so on. Of particular interest is what happens to demand when one or more of these variables change. This variation can be measured using differentiation, so we need to extend this concept to include functions of several variables. Marginal functions and elasticity can then be determined and analysed.

In Chapter 3, we saw how to find the maximum and minimum values of a function of one variable. For functions of two or more variables there are two different types of problem to consider: unconstrained and constrained. Unconstrained problems involve the optimisation of functions in which the variables are free to take any values whatsoever. In a constrained problem only certain combinations of the variables are examined.

 Revision checklist

What you need to know:

❑ how to work out the first- and second-order partial derivatives of functions of several variables;

❑ the small increments formula;

❑ how to find marginal products for production functions and utility functions, including the calculation of MRTS and MRCS;

❑ the formula for partial elasticity;

❑ how to find, and classify, stationary points of functions of two variables;

❑ how to solve constrained optimisation problems using the substitution and Lagrange multiplier methods.

✳ Assessment advice

● Practise finding partial derivatives so that you reach the stage when the process becomes second nature.

● Learn the formulae for calculating MRTS and MRCS, making sure you know which marginal product is on the top and bottom of each one.

- Make sure you can interpret the values of all marginal concepts and elasticity.
- Don't forget to classify the stationary points of an unconstrained optimisation problem after you have found them.
- There are two methods of solving a constrained optimisation problem. If you are given a free choice of method, think ahead and pick the one that involves the simpler algebra.
- Remember that the numerical value of the Lagrange multiplier gives the approximate change in the optimal value of the objective function when the constraint increases by one unit.

✱ Assessment question

Could you answer this question? Guidelines on answering the question are presented at the end of this chapter.

A firm's unit capital and labour costs are £1 and £2, respectively, and the total input costs are fixed at £M. If the production function is given by $Q = 8KL$, use the method of Lagrange multipliers to show that the optimal output is M^2 and find the levels of K and L at which it is achieved.

(a) Verify that the ratio of marginal product to price is the same for both inputs at the optimum, and give an interpretation of this result.

(b) Verify that the Lagrange multiplier gives the approximate change in the optimal output when the input costs increase by one unit.

(c) Write down the equation of the isoquant that passes through the optimum point, and hence show that the cost constraint is a tangent to the isoquant at the optimum. Explain why this is to be expected.

Partial differentiation

Given a function of two variables, $z = f(x, y)$, it is possible to determine two first-order derivatives.

Key definitions

The **partial derivative of f with respect to x** is denoted by

$$\frac{\partial f}{\partial x}$$

or

$$\frac{\partial z}{\partial x}$$

or f_x and is found by differentiating f with respect to x, with y held constant.

The **partial derivative of f with respect to y** is denoted by

$$\frac{\partial f}{\partial y}$$

or

$$\frac{\partial z}{\partial y}$$

or f_y and is found by differentiating f with respect to y, with x held constant.

To find the partial derivative of $z = xy^3 + 2x^2 + 6y$ with respect to x, we regard x as the variable and treat y as a constant. We know from Chapter 3 that we can differentiate term-by-term, so we consider these separately.

First term xy^3: a constant multiple of x, such as cx, differentiates to give the constant c, so if we treat y^3 as a constant then the first term differentiates to y^3.

Second term $2x^2$: can be differentiated in the normal way to give $4x$.

Third term $6y$: if y is held fixed then $6y$ is a constant, which differentiates to zero.

Hence

$$\frac{\partial z}{\partial x} = y^3 + 4x + 0 = y^3 + 4x.$$

To find the partial derivative of $z = xy^3 + 2x^2 + 6y$ with respect to y, we regard y as the variable and treat x as a constant, which gives

$$\frac{\partial z}{\partial y} = 3xy^2 + 0 + 6 = 3xy^2 + 6.$$

Partial derivatives give the approximate change in z brought about by a one-unit increase in x or y when the other variable is fixed. To illustrate this, suppose you wanted to estimate the change in the previous example, $z = xy^3 + 2x^2 + 6y$, as x changes from 2 to 2.1, with y fixed at 3. We first evaluate the partial derivative, $\partial z/\partial x$ at (2, 3):

$$\frac{\partial z}{\partial x} = 3^3 + 4 \times 2 = 35$$

and then multiply this by the change, $\Delta x = 0.1$, to get 3.5.

Similarly, if y changes from 3 to 2.9, with x fixed at 2, we evaluate $\partial z/\partial y$ at (2, 3):

$$\frac{\partial z}{\partial y} = 3 \times 2 \times 3^2 + 6 = 60.$$

This gives the approximate change in z brought about by a one-unit change in y, so when $\Delta y = -0.1$, the change in z is about -6.

Of course, if x and y both change, then the total change in z can be found by summing the individual changes. In this case, $\Delta z \approx 3.5 - 6 = -2.5$.

In general,

$$\Delta z \approx \frac{\partial z}{\partial x} \times \Delta x + \frac{\partial z}{\partial y} \times \Delta y$$

(*small increments formula*), where the partial derivatives are evaluated at the original point.

Although this is only an approximation, the error diminishes as Δx and Δy tend to zero, so the formula is sometimes written as the equation

$$dz = \frac{\partial z}{\partial x} \times dx + \frac{\partial z}{\partial y} \times dy$$

(where dx, dy, dz are called *differentials*).

Test yourself

Q1. If $z = x^2y + 10y - 4x$, evaluate $\partial z/\partial x$ and $\partial z/\partial y$ at (3, 5), and hence estimate the change in z when x increases by 0.2 and y decreases by 0.1.

Second-order derivatives can be found in an analogous way. We write

$$\frac{\partial^2 f}{\partial x^2} \quad \text{or}$$

$$\frac{\partial^2 z}{\partial x^2} \quad \text{or } f_{xx}$$

for the function obtained by differentiating twice with respect to x

$$\frac{\partial^2 f}{\partial y^2} \quad \text{or}$$

$$\frac{\partial^2 z}{\partial y^2} \quad \text{or } f_{yy}$$

for the function obtained by differentiating twice with respect to y

$$\frac{\partial^2 f}{\partial x \, \partial y} \quad \text{or}$$

$$\frac{\partial^2 z}{\partial x \, \partial y} \quad \text{or } f_{xy}$$

for the function obtained by differentiating with respect to x and y.

Strictly speaking, f_{xy} denotes the function obtained by differentiating first with respect to y and then with respect to x, with f_{yx} used for the reverse order. However, for all functions that you are likely to meet in economics, you get the same expression irrespective of the order in which you perform the differentiation (*Young's theorem*), so it makes no difference which you do first.

For the previous example, $z = xy^3 + 2x^2 + 6y$, we could partially differentiate

$$\frac{\partial z}{\partial x} = y^3 + 4x$$

with respect to y to get

$$\frac{\partial^2 z}{\partial y \, \partial x} = 3y^2$$

or partially differentiate

$$\frac{\partial z}{\partial y} = 3xy^2 + 6$$

with respect to x to get

$$\frac{\partial^2 z}{\partial x \, \partial y} = 3y^2,$$

which is the same answer.

So far we have concentrated on functions of two variables but the mathematics extend to functions of more variables.

Worked example

Find expressions for f_1, f_{31}, f_2, f_{22} for the function

$$f(x_1, x_2, x_3) = x_1 x_2 x_3 - 4x_2^5 x_3 + x_2 x_3^7.$$

Solution

$$f_1 = \frac{\partial f}{\partial x_1} = x_2 x_3$$

so

$$f_{31} = \frac{\partial^2 f}{\partial x_3 \, \partial x_1} = x_2.$$

$$f_2 = \frac{\partial f}{\partial x_2} = x_1 x_3 - 20x_2^4 x_3 + x_3^7$$

so

$$f_{22} = \frac{\partial^2 f}{\partial x_2^2} = -80x_2^3 x_3.$$

Test yourself

Q2. Find expressions for f_2, f_{33}, f_{13} for the function

$$f(x_1, x_2, x_3) = x_1^2 x_2 x_3 - 3x_2^2 x_3 + x_1 x_3^2 + 6x_2.$$

Marginal functions and partial elasticity

Production functions

In the long-run, the output of a production process, Q, depends both on capital, K, and labour, L, so we write $Q = f(K, L)$.

> ## Key definitions
>
> The first-order partial derivatives of Q with respect to K and L are called the **marginal product of capital** and **marginal product of labour**, and are denoted by MP_K and MP_L, respectively.

These can be interpreted in the usual way. For example, the marginal product of labour gives the approximate change in output brought about by a one-unit increase in L when K is held fixed.

A production function that is used frequently in economic analysis is the *Cobb-Douglas production function*, $Q = AL^{\alpha}K^{\beta}$, where A, α and β are constants with $A > 0$, $0 < \alpha < 1$ and $0 < \beta < 1$.

Worked example

Find expressions for $\partial Q/\partial L$ and $\partial^2 Q/\partial L^2$ for the general Cobb-Douglas production function and deduce that

(a) the law of diminishing returns holds;

(b) the marginal product of labour is less than the average product of labour.

Solution

The first- and second-order partial derivatives of Q with respect to L are:

$$\frac{\partial Q}{\partial L} = A\alpha L^{\alpha-1}K^{\beta}$$

and

$$\frac{\partial^2 Q}{\partial L^2} = A\alpha(\alpha - 1)L^{\alpha-2}K^{\beta}.$$

(a) The first of these is MP_L, and the second is the derivative of MP_L with respect to L, with K held constant. All factors in the expression for $\partial^2 Q/\partial L^2$ are positive, with the exception of $\alpha - 1$, which is negative because $\alpha < 1$. Hence $\partial^2 Q/\partial L^2 < 0$, showing that MP_L decreases as labour input, L, increases, so the law of diminishing returns holds.

(b) The average product of labour, AP_L, is defined as total output divided by the number of units of labour so that

$$AP_L = \frac{Q}{L} = \frac{AL^{\alpha}K^{\beta}}{L} = AL^{\alpha-1}K^{\beta}.$$

Comparing this with the expression for MP_L above, we see that $MP_L = \alpha(AP_L)$.

Hence $MP_L < AP_L$ because $0 < \alpha < 1$.

In theory, it is possible to represent a function of two variables by a surface in three dimensions. However, in practice, this is not at all easy, so instead we draw two-dimensional curves called *isoquants*. These are curves indicating all possible combinations of the two factors that give the same level of output. For example, for the production function

$$Q = 20K^{\frac{1}{2}}L^{\frac{1}{2}} \tag{5.1}$$

the output is 80 when $L = 2$, $K = 8$ and $L = 4$, $K = 4$ and $L = 8$, $K = 2$ and so on. The points (2, 8), (4, 4) and (8, 2) lie on the same isoquant whereas (4, 9) lies on a different isoquant because this combination of input values yields an output of 120. This is illustrated in Figure 5.1. It is possible to obtain the mathematical equation for each curve shown in Figure 5.1 by simply rearranging Equation 5.1 to make K the subject. If the output is 80, then

$$20K^{\frac{1}{2}}L^{\frac{1}{2}} = 80$$

$$K^{\frac{1}{2}} = \frac{4}{L^{\frac{1}{2}}} \quad \text{(divide both sides by } 20L^{\frac{1}{2}}\text{)}$$

$$K = \frac{16}{L} \quad \text{(square both sides)}.$$

The shape of each curve is the same, which is to be expected. If at any point labour decreases, you need to increase capital in order to maintain the same level of production. Figure 5.1 shows that the extra capital varies along the curve. If L is already fairly low then to lose one unit of labour is likely to be significant and you need to increase K considerably to compensate. This exchange of labour for capital can be quantified.

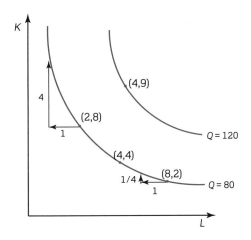

Figure 5.1

Key definition

The **marginal rate of technical substitution** (MRTS) is the amount by which capital needs to rise to maintain a constant level of output when labour decreases by one unit.

This "one-unit-change" idea is one that we met before in Chapter 3, and we can estimate the value using differentiation. From Figure 5.1, we see that MRTS can be measured as the gradient of an isoquant:

$$MRTS = -\frac{dK}{dL}$$

where the change of sign is introduced deliberately to make the answer positive.

For the curve $K = 16L^{-1}$,

$$\frac{dK}{dL} = -16L^{-2}$$

so at the point (2, 8), $MRTS = 4$, as shown in Figure 5.1.

It is possible to work out the value of MRTS without actually obtaining an expression for K in terms of L. The differential version of the small-increments formula gives

$$dQ = \frac{\partial Q}{\partial K} \times dK + \frac{\partial Q}{\partial L} \times dL.$$

Along an isoquant, output remains fixed so $dQ = 0$, and this formula can be used to show that

$$\frac{dK}{dL} = -\frac{\partial Q/\partial L}{\partial Q/\partial K} = -\frac{MP_L}{MP_K}.$$

As $MRTS = -\dfrac{dK}{dL}$,

we have the alternative formula

$$MRTS = \frac{MP_L}{MP_K}.$$

For the Cobb-Douglas production function, $Q = 20K^{\frac{1}{2}}L^{\frac{1}{2}}$,

$MP_K = 10K^{-\frac{1}{2}}L^{\frac{1}{2}}$ and $MP_L = 10K^{\frac{1}{2}}L^{-\frac{1}{2}}$. So

$$MRTS = \frac{10K^{\frac{1}{2}}L^{-\frac{1}{2}}}{10K^{-\frac{1}{2}}L^{\frac{1}{2}}} = \frac{K}{L}.$$

As a check, at the point (2, 8),

$$MRTS = \frac{8}{2} = 4,$$

which agrees with the value obtained previously.

Utility functions

The mathematical argument used for a production function can be applied to a utility function, $U = f(x, y)$, which measures the satisfaction that a consumer gains from buying x units of good X and y units of good Y. Marginal utilities for each good are defined as

$$MU_X = \frac{\partial U}{\partial x}$$

and

$$MU_Y = \frac{\partial U}{\partial y}$$

and give the change in utility brought about by a one-unit increase in X and Y, respectively. *Indifference curves* are analogous to isoquants and consist of all points (x, y) that give the same value of utility. A typical indifference map looks the same as Figure 5.1 and the *marginal rate of commodity substitution* (MRCS) gives the increase in consumption of good Y needed to maintain a particular level of satisfaction when the consumption of X goes down by one unit. As expected, MRCS can be found from

$$MRCS = -\frac{dy}{dx} = \frac{MU_X}{MU_Y}.$$

Test yourself

Q3. A utility function is given by $U = 60x^{\frac{1}{3}}y^{\frac{1}{2}}$.

(a) Obtain expressions for the marginal utilities MU_X and MU_Y.

(b) Find the value of *MRCS* at the point (8, 9), and hence estimate the increase in the consumption of good X needed to maintain the current level of satisfaction when Y decreases by two units.

Elasticity of demand

In the real world, the demand, Q, for a firm's product depends on several factors, not just the (own) price, P, of the good. These may include the price of an alternative good, P_A, and consumer income, Y, so that the demand function takes the form $Q = f(P, P_A, Y, \ldots)$.

Key definitions

Price elasticity of demand measures the responsiveness of demand to changes in (own) price when all other variables are fixed:

$$\frac{P}{Q} \times \frac{\partial Q}{\partial P}.$$

Cross-price elasticity of demand measures the responsiveness of demand to changes in the price of the alternative good when all other variables are fixed:

$$\frac{P_A}{Q} \times \frac{\partial Q}{\partial P_A}.$$

Income elasticity of demand measures the responsiveness of demand to changes in income when all other variables are fixed:

$$\frac{Y}{Q} \times \frac{\partial Q}{\partial Y}.$$

Worked example

The demand function for a good is given by $Q = 130 - 4P - 0.1P_A^2 + 2Y$.

Find the price, cross-price and income elasticity of demand at $P = 20$, $P_A = 10$ and $Y = 5$.

Estimate the percentage change in demand when P_A increases by 5%. Are the goods substitutable or complementary?

Solution

The demand at these values is

$$Q = 130 - 4 \times 20 - 0.1 \times 10^2 + 2 \times 5 = 50.$$

The three first-order partial derivatives are:

$$\frac{\partial Q}{\partial P} = -4; \quad \frac{\partial Q}{\partial P_A} = -0.2P_A; \quad \frac{\partial Q}{\partial Y} = 2.$$

Price elasticity of demand $= \dfrac{P}{Q} \times \dfrac{\partial Q}{\partial P} = \dfrac{20}{50} \times (-4) = -1.6.$

Cross-price elasticity of demand $= \dfrac{P_A}{Q} \times \dfrac{\partial Q}{\partial P_A} = \dfrac{10}{50} \times (-2) = -0.4.$

Income elasticity of demand $= \dfrac{Y}{Q} \times \dfrac{\partial Q}{\partial Y} = \dfrac{5}{50} \times 2 = 0.2.$

The value of the cross-price elasticity of demand is -0.4 so

$$\dfrac{\text{percentage change in demand}}{\text{percentage change in price of alternative good}} = -0.4.$$

The percentage change in demand is $-0.4 \times 5 = -2\%.$

This is negative, so an increase in the price of the alternative good causes demand of the good to fall. The two goods are therefore complementary.

Test yourself

Q4. The demand function for a good is given by $Q = 100 - 4P + 3P_A - Y$.

Find the price, cross-price and income elasticity of demand at $P = 8$, $P_A = 12$ and $Y = 24$.

Estimate the percentage change in demand when Y increases by 5%. Is the good inferior or superior?

Optimisation

The stationary points (a, b) of a function $f(x, y)$ are found by solving the simultaneous equations $f_x(x, y) = 0$ and $f_y(x, y) = 0$.

If

- $f_{xx} > 0$, $f_{yy} > 0$ and $f_{xx}f_{yy} - f_{xy}^2 > 0$ at (a, b), then f has a minimum at (a, b);
- $f_{xx} < 0$, $f_{yy} < 0$ and $f_{xx}f_{yy} - f_{xy}^2 > 0$ at (a, b), then f has a maximum at (a, b);
- $f_{xx}f_{yy} - f_{xy}^2 < 0$ at (a, b), then f has a saddle point at (a, b).

Worked example

A firm produces two substitutable goods, X_1 and X_2. The demand for each good is given by $Q_1 = 400 - 2P_1 + P_2$ and $Q_2 = 280 + 3P_1 - 4P_2$.

What price should the firm charge for each good to maximise total revenue?

Solution

$$TR = TR_1 + TR_2$$
$$= P_1 Q_1 + P_2 Q_2$$
$$= P_1(400 - 2P_1 + P_2) + P_2(280 + 3P_1 - 4P_2)$$
$$= 400P_1 + 280P_2 + 4P_1 P_2 - 2P_1^2 - 4P_2^2$$

The stationary point is the solution of the simultaneous equations:

$$\frac{\partial(TR)}{\partial P_1} = 400 + 4P_2 - 4P_1 = 0 \Rightarrow P_1 - P_2 = 100$$

$$\frac{\partial(TR)}{\partial P_2} = 280 + 4P_1 - 8P_2 = 0 \Rightarrow -P_1 + 2P_2 = 70$$

Adding gives $P_2 = 170 \Rightarrow P_1 = 270$.

To classify the stationary point we need the second-order derivatives:

$$\frac{\partial^2(TR)}{\partial P_1^2} = -4 \quad \frac{\partial^2(TR)}{\partial P_2^2} = -8 \quad \frac{\partial^2(TR)}{\partial P_1 \partial P_2} = 4.$$

The first two of these are negative and

$$\left(\frac{\partial^2(TR)}{\partial P_1^2}\right)\left(\frac{\partial^2(TR)}{\partial P_2^2}\right) - \left(\frac{\partial^2(TR)}{\partial P_1 \partial P_2}\right)^2 = (-4)(-8) - 4^2 = 16 > 0$$

so the point is a maximum.

Test yourself

Q5. A company sells its product in two markets: EU and China. The demand function for the European market is $P_1 = 50 - 2Q_1$ and the demand function for the Chinese market is $P_2 = 80 - 3Q_2$. The total cost function is $TC = 500 + 10(Q_1 + Q_2)$. Determine the company's pricing policy that maximises profit.

In the previous worked example and Test Yourself question, the variables are free to take any values. This is unrealistic in many practical situations. Individual consumers do not have unlimited funds so they maximise their utility subject to a cost constraint. A firm wishing to minimise total input costs may well be contracted to supply a certain number of units of output. The general problem is to optimise an *objective function*, $z = f(x, y)$, subject to a *constraint*, $\varphi(x, y) = M$.

Worked example

An individual's utility function is given by $U = 2xy + x^2$, where x and y denote the number of items of two goods, X and Y. The prices of these goods are £3 and £2, respectively. Assuming that the individual has £84 available to spend on these goods, find the maximum value of U.

Estimate the new optimal utility if the amount available to spend increases by £1.

Solution

The problem is to maximise $U = 2xy + x^2$, subject to the budgetary constraint, $3x + 2y = 84$.

Method 1: substitution

For this method we use the constraint to express y in terms of x. Subtracting $3x$ from both sides and dividing by 2 gives $y = 42 - 1.5x$.

We now substitute this into U, which then becomes a function of just one variable,

$$U = 2x(42 - 1.5x) + x^2 = 84x - 2x^2 \qquad (5.2)$$

The problem can now be solved using the method described in Chapter 3.

The value of x that maximises utility is the solution of

$$\frac{dU}{dx} = 84 - 4x = 0,$$

which is 21.

The optimal value of U is obtained by substituting $x = 21$ into Equation 5.2, which gives $U = 882$.

The new optimal value of U can be found by repeating the calculations replacing £84 by £85 throughout. The utility function becomes $U = 85x - 2x^2$ and the solution of

$$\frac{dU}{dx} = 85 - 4x = 0$$

is now 21.25. The corresponding value of U is 903.125.

Method 2: Lagrange multiplier

A new function (the *Lagrangian*) is defined as

$g(x, y, \lambda) = f(x, y) + \lambda[M - \varphi(x, y)]$ where g is a function of the original variables, x and y, together with the Lagrange multiplier, λ.

The optimal solution is found by solving the simultaneous equations

$$\frac{\partial g}{\partial x} = 0, \quad \frac{\partial g}{\partial y} = 0, \quad \frac{\partial g}{\partial \lambda} = 0$$

for the three unknowns, x, y and λ.

In this case $g(x, y, \lambda) = 2xy + x^2 + \lambda[84 - 3x - 2y]$

$$\frac{\partial g}{\partial x} = 2y + 2x - 3\lambda = 0; \quad \frac{\partial g}{\partial y} = 2x - 2\lambda = 0; \quad \frac{\partial g}{\partial \lambda} = 84 - 3x - 2y = 0.$$

The second equation immediately gives $x = \lambda$, which can be substituted into the first equation to get $y = 0.5\lambda$. Substituting both of these in the third equation gives $84 - 4\lambda = 0$ with solution $\lambda = 21$.

The complete solution of the system of equations is $x = 21$, $y = 10.5$, $\lambda = 21$.

The optimal value of U is found by substituting the values of x and y into the utility function, which gives $U = 2 \times 21 \times 10.5 + 21^2 = 882$.

It is possible to give an interpretation of the value of the Lagrange multiplier itself. In general, it is the approximate change in the optimal value of the objective function due to a one-unit increase in the value of M. In this example $\lambda = 21$ so when the budget rises from £84 to £85, the value of U increases by approximately 21 to become $882 + 21 = 903$.

Test yourself

Q6. A firm's production function is given by $Q = 10K^{\frac{1}{2}}L^{\frac{1}{3}}$. Unit capital and labour costs are £1 and £4, respectively. Find the values of K and L that minimise total input costs if the firm is contracted to provide 200 units of output. Estimate the increase in total input costs if the firm is contracted to provide an additional 10 units of output.

Chapter summary – pulling it all together

By the end of this chapter you should be able to:

	Confident ✓	Not confident?
Know how to find partial derivatives and use the small increments formula		Revise pages 81–85
Solve problems involving production functions		Revise pages 85–89
Solve problems involving utility functions		Revise page 89
Calculate partial elasticities associated with a demand function		Revise pages 89–91
Solve unconstrained optimisation problems		Revise pages 91–92
Solve constrained optimisation problems		Revise pages 92–94

Now try the assessment question at the start of the chapter using the answer guidelines below.

Answer guidelines

✱ Assessment question

A firm's unit capital and labour costs are £1 and £2, respectively, and the total input costs are fixed at £M. If the production function is given by $Q = 8KL$, use the method of Lagrange multipliers to show that the optimal output is M^2, and find the levels of K and L at which it is achieved.

(a) Verify that the ratio of marginal product to price is the same for both inputs at the optimum, and give an interpretation of this result.

(b) Verify that the Lagrange multiplier gives the approximate change in the optimal output when the input costs increase by one unit.

(c) Write down the equation of the isoquant that passes through the optimum point and hence show that the cost constraint is a tangent to the isoquant at the optimum. Explain why this is to be expected.

Approaching the question

- In the first part of the question you need to optimise the output where the inputs are restricted by the fixed costs. This is a constrained optimisation problem and you are told to solve this by the Lagrange multiplier method. A similar worked example can be found on page 94.

- Part (a) uses the word "verify", so no formal mathematics is required. You are merely being asked to check that the two ratios are equal. You can think of it as a useful check that you haven't made any mistakes in the first part.

- Again in part (b), although the result itself is quite general, you are only asked to check it out for this particular problem. You will need the expressions for optimal output and the Lagrange multiplier obtained previously.

- Isoquant maps are considered on pages 87–89, which you may find helpful when tackling the last part of the question.

Method of solution

- The first thing to do is to write down the constraint. Each unit of capital costs £1 and each unit of labour costs £2. You want to use K and L units of each and the total is equal to M.

- There are two methods for solving constrained optimisation problems: substitution and Lagrange multipliers. For this question you are told to use the Lagrange multiplier method.
  - Write down the Lagrangian function, $g(K, L, \lambda)$.
  - Write down the first-order conditions,

$$\frac{\partial g}{\partial K} = 0, \frac{\partial g}{\partial L} = 0, \frac{\partial g}{\partial \lambda} = 0.$$

  - The last of these is just the original cost constraint.
  - The first two enable you to express L and K in terms of λ. These can be substituted into the third equation, which can be used to express λ in terms of M. This can then be substituted back to find K, L and Q in terms of M. You are told that $Q = M^2$, which provides a useful check.

- An important result in economic theory shows that when output is maximised subject to a cost constraint, the ratio of marginal product to price is the same for all inputs. You are not asked to give a general proof of this result, but merely to verify that it is true in this particular problem, and to give a brief statement about what this result means in economic terms.

- For part (b) you know that the optimal value of Q is M^2. Replace M by $M + 1$ to investigate the change in Q. This answer can then be compared with the value of λ.

- For part (c) replace the letter Q by the optimal output found in part (a), and then rearrange to express K in terms of L. You can evaluate the gradients of the isoquant and cost line, and verify that they are the same at the optimal point.

- For the very last part of (c) you need to explain why the cost line is a tangent to the isoquant at the optimum. To do this draw the cost constraint line on an isoquant map, and remember that the output increases as the isoquants get further away from the origin.

Companion website

Go to the companion website at **www.pearsoned.co.uk/econexpress** to find more revision support online for this topic area.

Notes

6 Linear mathematics

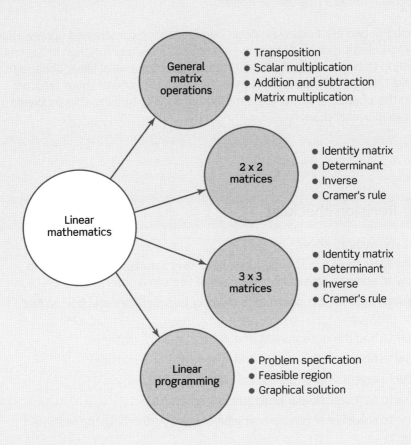

A printable version of this topic map is available from **www.pearsoned.co.uk/econexpress**

Introduction

The simplest mathematical models of economic behaviour assume that the relationships between variables are linear. Although modelling supply and demand as two linear functions may not be an accurate representation of what happens in the real world, it does provide a first approximation to the truth. It also makes the mathematical analysis relatively straightforward. In this chapter we focus on two topics that are used to solve linear problems: matrices and linear programming.

Matrices are rectangular arrays of numbers enclosed by a pair of brackets. We will use round brackets in this book but square brackets are also acceptable. Matrix inverses can be used to solve systems of linear equations that arise in both macro- and microeconomics. If only a few of the variables need to be found, then Cramer's rule can be applied.

In Chapter 5, two methods were described for solving constrained optimisation problems: substitution and Lagrange multipliers. If a linear function of several variables is to be maximised or minimised, subject to several linear constraints that take the form of inequalities, then the problem is one of linear programming. In this chapter we describe a method of solving two-variable problems using a graphical approach.

 Revision checklist

What you need to know:

- ❑ how to multiply a matrix by a number, how to transpose a matrix and how to add or subtract two matrices of the same order;
- ❑ recognise when it is possible to multiply two matrices and how to find the product;
- ❑ how to find the determinant and inverse of 2 × 2 matrices;
- ❑ how to find the determinant and inverse of 3 × 3 matrices;
- ❑ how to use Cramer's rule to find individual variables;
- ❑ how to formulate linear programming problems;
- ❑ how to solve linear programming problems by sketching the feasible region.

Assessment advice

- Remember that you can only add or subtract matrices if they have the same order.
- Remember that you can only work out a matrix product, **AB**, if the number of columns of **A** is the same as the number of rows of **B**.
- When finding the inverse of a matrix, don't forget to divide by the determinant. If the determinant is zero the inverse does not exist.
- When finding the inverse of a 2 × 2 matrix, you swap the two numbers on the leading diagonal, but do *not* swap the off-diagonals. You change the signs of the off-diagonals instead.
- Be patient when finding the inverse of a 3 × 3 matrix. As a check on your final answer, multiply your inverse by the original matrix. You should get the identity matrix.
- When formulating linear programming problems, remember to state exactly what the variables represent, if they have not been specified in the question.
- It pays to think ahead and choose a sensible scale when drawing the feasible region. Try to fill the page but make sure that your lines are going to fit.

 Assessment question

Could you answer this question? Guidelines on answering the question are presented at the end of this chapter.

(a)   Use a matrix method to solve the following simultaneous equations:

$$4x + 3y = 900$$
$$5x + 7y = 1750.$$

Give your answers as fractions.

(b)   A food supplier makes two different varieties of smoothie, "Exotic" and "Floridian", which it sells in 2-litre cartons. The main ingredients and profit made on each carton are as follows:

	Banana	Mango	Orange	Profit
Exotic	4	2	5	£2.25
Floridian	3	1	7	£2.00

The company has 900 bananas, 400 mangoes and 1,750 oranges to use, and wishes to arrange production to maximise total profit. It can sell all of the smoothies that it produces.

    (i)   Formulate this as a linear programming problem.

    (ii) Sketch the feasible region.

    (iii) Write down the exact coordinates of the corners of the region.

    (iv) Find the optimising production levels of each type of smoothie.

General matrix operations

Key definitions

A matrix with m rows and n columns is said to have **order m × n** (which is read "m by n").

A matrix with one row (or column) is called a row (or column) **vector**.

Provided two matrices have the same order, they can be added (or subtracted) in an obvious way, by simply adding (or subtracting) their corresponding elements:

$$\begin{pmatrix} 2 & 5 \\ 3 & -4 \\ -1 & 9 \end{pmatrix} + \begin{pmatrix} -1 & 7 \\ 0 & 2 \\ -5 & -3 \end{pmatrix} = \begin{pmatrix} 1 & 12 \\ 3 & -2 \\ -6 & 6 \end{pmatrix}$$

$$\begin{pmatrix} -3 & 2 & 0 & 8 \\ 1 & 6 & -4 & 2 \end{pmatrix} - \begin{pmatrix} -2 & 0 & 5 & 6 \\ -4 & 7 & 1 & 1 \end{pmatrix} = \begin{pmatrix} -1 & 2 & -5 & 2 \\ 5 & -1 & -5 & 1 \end{pmatrix}$$

The order of the result is the same as that of the original pair of matrices.

It is possible to multiply a matrix by a number just by scaling each element:

$$3 \times \begin{pmatrix} 1 & -3 & 5 & 8 \\ 6 & 4 & -1 & 0 \\ 2 & 0 & 9 & -3 \end{pmatrix} = \begin{pmatrix} 3 & -9 & 15 & 24 \\ 18 & 12 & -3 & 0 \\ 6 & 0 & 27 & -9 \end{pmatrix}$$

Again, the order of the matrix is unchanged.

The *transpose* of a matrix is obtained by interchanging rows with columns, so the transpose of

$$A = \begin{pmatrix} 2 & 4 \\ 9 & 3 \\ 5 & 7 \end{pmatrix}$$

is

$$A^T = \begin{pmatrix} 2 & 9 & 5 \\ 4 & 3 & 7 \end{pmatrix}.$$

(the transpose is sometimes written A').

If a matrix has order $m \times n$ then its transpose has order $n \times m$.

Test yourself

Q1. Let

$$A = \begin{pmatrix} 4 & -2 & 9 \\ 3 & 10 & 5 \end{pmatrix}, B = \begin{pmatrix} 0 & 2 & 9 \\ 3 & 2 & -3 \\ 7 & 1 & 4 \end{pmatrix} \text{ and } C = \begin{pmatrix} 6 & 1 & 0 \\ -6 & 5 & 3 \end{pmatrix}.$$

(a) State the orders of each of the above matrices.

(b) Work out each of the following, where possible:

$$A + B, \quad 2B, \quad C^T, \quad (A - C)^T.$$

It is only possible work out the matrix product, **AB**, when the number of columns of **A** matches the number of rows of **B**. The number of rows in the answer is the same as the number of rows of **A**, and the number of columns in the answer is the same as the number of columns of **B**:

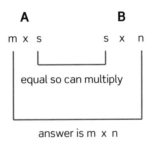

A   B

m x s   s x n

equal so can multiply

answer is m x n

Worked example

Work out the matrix product, **AB**, when

$$A = \begin{pmatrix} 1 & 2 & -3 & 5 \\ 8 & 0 & 4 & -2 \\ -3 & 4 & 6 & -7 \end{pmatrix} \text{ and } B = \begin{pmatrix} 9 & 2 \\ -2 & 0 \\ 7 & 4 \\ -1 & -1 \end{pmatrix}$$

Solution

It is possible to form the product **AB** since **A** has four columns and **B** has the same number of rows. Also, **AB** has order 3 × 2 because **A** has 3 rows and **B** has 2 columns:

$$
\begin{array}{cc}
\mathbf{A} & \mathbf{B} \\
3 \times 4 & 4 \times 2
\end{array}
$$

equal so can multiply

answer is 3 × 2

$$
\begin{pmatrix} 1 & 2 & -3 & 5 \\ 8 & 0 & 4 & -2 \\ -3 & 4 & 6 & -7 \end{pmatrix} \begin{pmatrix} 9 & 2 \\ -2 & 0 \\ 7 & 4 \\ -1 & -1 \end{pmatrix} = \begin{pmatrix} a & b \\ c & d \\ e & f \end{pmatrix}
$$

The element a is in the first row and first column so we take the first row of **A** and the first column of **B**, and multiply them together:

$$
a = (1 \quad 2 \quad -3 \quad 5) \begin{pmatrix} 9 \\ -2 \\ 7 \\ -1 \end{pmatrix} = -21
$$

since $1 \times 9 + 2 \times (-2) + (-3) \times 7 + 5 \times (-1) = -21$.

The remaining five elements are worked out similarly. For example, the element f is in the third row and second column so we take the third row of **A**, the second column of **B** and multiply them together:

$$
f = (-3 \quad 4 \quad 6 \quad -7) \begin{pmatrix} 2 \\ 0 \\ 4 \\ -1 \end{pmatrix} = 25
$$

since $(-3) \times 2 + 4 \times 0 + 6 \times 4 + (-7) \times (-1) = 25$.

You can check that the final answer is given by

$$
\begin{pmatrix} 1 & 2 & -3 & 5 \\ 8 & 0 & 4 & -2 \\ -3 & 4 & 6 & -7 \end{pmatrix} \begin{pmatrix} 9 & 2 \\ -2 & 0 \\ 7 & 4 \\ -1 & -1 \end{pmatrix} = \begin{pmatrix} -21 & -15 \\ 102 & 34 \\ 14 & 25 \end{pmatrix}.
$$

Q2. If the orders of matrices **A**, **B** and **C** are 2 × 3, 4 × 3 and 4 × 2, respectively, decide which of the following matrix products are possible. If the calculation is possible, state the order of the resulting matrix:

(a) **AB**

(b) **AC**

(c) **CA**

(d) **AB**ᵀ

(e) **C**ᵀ**BA**ᵀ

Q3. Work out the matrix product **AB** in the case when

$$\mathbf{A} = \begin{pmatrix} 1 & -2 \\ 3 & -1 \\ 6 & 4 \end{pmatrix} \text{ and } \mathbf{B} = \begin{pmatrix} 6 & 4 & -1 & 2 \\ 1 & 3 & 0 & 5 \end{pmatrix}$$

Q4. If $\mathbf{I} = \begin{pmatrix} 1 & 0 \\ 0 & 1 \end{pmatrix}$, $\mathbf{A} = \begin{pmatrix} a & b \\ c & d \end{pmatrix}$, $\mathbf{x} = \begin{pmatrix} x \\ y \end{pmatrix}$ work out the matrix products,

AI, **IA**, **Ix** and **Ax**.

2 × 2 matrices

In this section we describe matrix methods for solving systems of two simultaneous linear equations in two unknowns.

Key definition

The matrix $\mathbf{I} = \begin{pmatrix} 1 & 0 \\ 0 & 1 \end{pmatrix}$ is the 2 × 2 **identity matrix** with the property that **AI = IA = A**.

If **A** and **B** are 2 × 2 matrices with the property that **AB = I** and **BA = I** then **B** is the **inverse** of **A** and we write **B = A**⁻¹.

The inverse of a 2 × 2 matrix, $\mathbf{A} = \begin{pmatrix} a & b \\ c & d \end{pmatrix}$, may be found in three easy steps:

Step 1	Swap the leading diagonal elements, a and d.
Step 2	Change the signs of the off-diagonal elements, b and c.
Step 3	Divide each element by the *determinant* $|\mathbf{A}| = ad - bc$.

Notice that the last step is impossible if $ad - bc = 0$. Matrices with this property are said to be singular and these matrices do not have an inverse.

Worked example

Find the inverse of the matrix $\mathbf{A} = \begin{pmatrix} 7 & 6 \\ 3 & 4 \end{pmatrix}$ and hence solve the following simultaneous equations:

$$7x + 6y = 5$$
$$3x + 4y = -1.$$

Solution

Step 1 Swap the numbers 7 and 4 to get $\begin{pmatrix} 4 & 6 \\ 3 & 7 \end{pmatrix}$.

Step 2 Change the sign of 3 and 6 to get $\begin{pmatrix} 4 & -6 \\ -3 & 7 \end{pmatrix}$.

Step 3 Divide by the determinant, $7 \times 4 - 6 \times 3 = 10$, to get

$$\mathbf{A}^{-1} = \frac{1}{10}\begin{pmatrix} 4 & -6 \\ -3 & 7 \end{pmatrix} = \begin{pmatrix} 0.4 & -0.6 \\ -0.3 & 0.7 \end{pmatrix}.$$

As a check, notice that

$$\mathbf{A}\mathbf{A}^{-1} = \begin{pmatrix} 7 & 6 \\ 3 & 4 \end{pmatrix}\begin{pmatrix} 0.4 & -0.6 \\ -0.3 & 0.7 \end{pmatrix} = \begin{pmatrix} 1 & 0 \\ 0 & 1 \end{pmatrix} = \mathbf{I}.$$

To solve the simultaneous equations

$$7x + 6y = 5$$
$$3x + 4y = -1$$

first express them in matrix form:

$$\begin{pmatrix} 7 & 6 \\ 3 & 4 \end{pmatrix}\begin{pmatrix} x \\ y \end{pmatrix} = \begin{pmatrix} 5 \\ -1 \end{pmatrix}$$

that is, $\mathbf{A}\mathbf{x} = \mathbf{b}$ where $\mathbf{x} = \begin{pmatrix} x \\ y \end{pmatrix}$ and $\mathbf{b} = \begin{pmatrix} 5 \\ -1 \end{pmatrix}$.

Multiplying both sides on the left by $\mathbf{A}^{-1}$ gives

$$\mathbf{A}^{-1}\mathbf{A}\mathbf{x} = \mathbf{A}^{-1}\mathbf{b}$$

$$\mathbf{I}\mathbf{x} = \mathbf{A}^{-1}\mathbf{b} \text{ (since } \mathbf{A}^{-1}\mathbf{A} = \mathbf{I})$$

$\mathbf{x} = \mathbf{A}^{-1}\mathbf{b}$ (since $\mathbf{Ix} = \mathbf{x}$)

so that

$$\begin{pmatrix} x \\ y \end{pmatrix} = \begin{pmatrix} 0.4 & -0.6 \\ -0.3 & 0.7 \end{pmatrix}\begin{pmatrix} 5 \\ -1 \end{pmatrix} = \begin{pmatrix} 2.6 \\ -2.2 \end{pmatrix}.$$

Hence $x = 2.6$ and $y = -2.2$.

Test yourself

Q5. The prices of two interdependent commodities satisfy the simultaneous equations

$$9P_1 + 5P_2 = 71$$
$$5P_1 + 3P_2 = 41.$$

Express this system in matrix notation and hence find the values of P_1 and P_2.

If you only need to find one of the two variables in the system

$$\begin{pmatrix} a & b \\ c & d \end{pmatrix}\begin{pmatrix} x \\ y \end{pmatrix} = \begin{pmatrix} e \\ f \end{pmatrix},$$

then the following formulae may be used:

$$x = \frac{\begin{vmatrix} e & b \\ f & d \end{vmatrix}}{\begin{vmatrix} a & b \\ c & d \end{vmatrix}}$$

and

$$y = \frac{\begin{vmatrix} a & e \\ c & f \end{vmatrix}}{\begin{vmatrix} a & b \\ c & d \end{vmatrix}}$$

(Cramer's rule)

The value of x is found by dividing one determinant by another. The matrix on the bottom is the original coefficient matrix. The one on the top is found by replacing the *first* column by the right-hand-side vector. The formula for y is similar but with the *second* column replaced by the right-hand-side vector. For the previous worked example,

$$\begin{pmatrix} 7 & 6 \\ 3 & 4 \end{pmatrix} \begin{pmatrix} x \\ y \end{pmatrix} = \begin{pmatrix} 5 \\ -1 \end{pmatrix},$$

Cramer's rule gives

$$x = \frac{\begin{vmatrix} 5 & 6 \\ -1 & 4 \end{vmatrix}}{\begin{vmatrix} 7 & 6 \\ 3 & 4 \end{vmatrix}} = \frac{5 \times 4 - 6 \times (-1)}{7 \times 4 - 6 \times 3} = \frac{26}{10} = 2.6$$

which agrees with the previous answer found using matrix inverses. You might like to check that Cramer's rule also gives the correct value for y.

Test yourself

Q6. The equilibrium levels of consumption, C, and income, Y, in a two-sector macroeconomic model satisfy

$$\begin{pmatrix} 1 & -1 \\ -a & 1 \end{pmatrix} \begin{pmatrix} Y \\ C \end{pmatrix} = \begin{pmatrix} I^* \\ b \end{pmatrix}.$$

Use Cramer's rule to express Y in terms of I^*, a and b.

---

3 × 3 matrices

In this section, we extend the ideas of the previous section to 3 × 3 matrices. The identity matrix is $\begin{pmatrix} 1 & 0 & 0 \\ 0 & 1 & 0 \\ 0 & 0 & 1 \end{pmatrix}$ and the inverse of the 3 × 3 matrix,

$A = \begin{pmatrix} a & b & c \\ d & e & f \\ g & h & i \end{pmatrix}$, is found in three steps.

Step 1

Form the matrix of *cofactors*, $\begin{pmatrix} A & B & C \\ D & E & F \\ G & H & I \end{pmatrix}$.

The cofactor of an element is the determinant of the 2 × 2 matrix left when the row and column containing that element are removed multiplied by +1 or −1 according to the following pattern:

$$\begin{pmatrix} + & - & + \\ - & + & - \\ + & - & + \end{pmatrix}.$$

Step 2

Transpose the matrix obtained in Step 1.

Step 3

Divide each element by the determinant, $|\mathbf{A}| = aA + bB + cC$.

Worked example

Use matrices to solve the following simultaneous equations:

$2x + 3y - 6z = 6$

$3x + 2y - 4z = 9$

$5x - 7y + z = 2$

Solution

In matrix notation the equations can be written as

$$\begin{pmatrix} 2 & 3 & -6 \\ 3 & 2 & -4 \\ 5 & -7 & 1 \end{pmatrix} \begin{pmatrix} x \\ y \\ z \end{pmatrix} = \begin{pmatrix} 6 \\ 9 \\ 2 \end{pmatrix}.$$

Step 1

The element $a = 2$, located in the top left-hand corner, is in the first row and first column. When this row and column are removed we are left with the 2 × 2 matrix $\begin{pmatrix} 2 & -4 \\ -7 & 1 \end{pmatrix}$, which has determinant −26.

According to the pattern of + and − mentioned earlier, we see that there is a + in the top left-hand corner. There is no need to change the sign of the determinant, so the cofactor, A = −26.

The element $b = 3$, located in the middle of the top row, is in the first row and second column. When this row and column are removed, we are left with the 2 × 2 matrix $\begin{pmatrix} 3 & -4 \\ 5 & 1 \end{pmatrix}$, which has determinant 23.

According the pattern of + and − mentioned earlier, we see that there is a − in the middle of the top row, so in this case we change the sign of the determinant to give the cofactor, B = −23.

The process continues with the remaining seven cofactors, which are then arranged as a 3 × 3 matrix, $\begin{pmatrix} -26 & -23 & -31 \\ 39 & 32 & 29 \\ 0 & -10 & -5 \end{pmatrix}$.

Step 2

The transpose of the matrix in Step 1 is $\begin{pmatrix} -26 & 39 & 0 \\ -23 & 32 & -10 \\ -31 & 29 & -5 \end{pmatrix}$.

Step 3

The determinant is worked out by multiplying each of the three elements in the top row by their cofactors and adding together:

$|\mathbf{A}| = 2 \times (-26) + 3 \times (-23) + (-6) \times (-31) = 65.$

So the inverse matrix is

$$\mathbf{A}^{-1} = \frac{1}{65} \begin{pmatrix} -26 & 39 & 0 \\ -23 & 32 & -10 \\ -31 & 29 & -5 \end{pmatrix}.$$

Finally we can obtain the solution of the simultaneous equations by multiplying the right-hand side vector by the inverse matrix:

$$\begin{pmatrix} x \\ y \\ z \end{pmatrix} = \frac{1}{65} \begin{pmatrix} -26 & 39 & 0 \\ -23 & 32 & -10 \\ -31 & 29 & -5 \end{pmatrix} \begin{pmatrix} 6 \\ 9 \\ 2 \end{pmatrix} = \begin{pmatrix} 3 \\ 2 \\ 1 \end{pmatrix}$$

so that x = 3, y = 2 and z = 1.

In this example, the determinant was worked out by expanding along the first row using the formula $|\mathbf{A}| = aA + bB + cC$.

In fact, it makes no difference which row or column is chosen. The formula for the second row would be $|\mathbf{A}| = dD + eE + fF$, which, in this case, gives $3 \times 39 + 2 \times 32 + (-4) \times 29 = 65$. The formula for the first column would be $|\mathbf{A}| = aA + dD + gG$, which gives $2 \times (-26) + 3 \times 39 + 0 \times (-31) = 65$.

In practice, you would choose any row or column containing one or more zeros to minimise the amount of work required, particularly if you only need to find the determinant rather than the inverse matrix. This is illustrated in the following example, in which Cramer's rule is used to find only one of the variables in the system.

Worked example

Use Cramer's rule to find z in the system

$$\begin{pmatrix} 2 & 3 & -6 \\ 3 & 2 & -4 \\ 5 & -7 & 1 \end{pmatrix} \begin{pmatrix} x \\ y \\ z \end{pmatrix} = \begin{pmatrix} 13 \\ 0 \\ 0 \end{pmatrix}.$$

Solution

Cramer's rule gives

$$z = \dfrac{\begin{vmatrix} 2 & 3 & 13 \\ 3 & 2 & 0 \\ 5 & -7 & 0 \end{vmatrix}}{\begin{vmatrix} 2 & 3 & -6 \\ 3 & 2 & -4 \\ 5 & -7 & 1 \end{vmatrix}}.$$

The determinant on the bottom of this fraction has already been calculated to be 65 in the previous example.

For the determinant on the top, notice that there are two zeros in the last column, so we expand down this column:

$$\begin{vmatrix} 2 & 3 & 13 \\ 3 & 2 & 0 \\ 5 & -7 & 0 \end{vmatrix} = 13 \begin{vmatrix} 3 & 2 \\ 5 & -7 \end{vmatrix} - 0 \begin{vmatrix} 2 & 3 \\ 5 & -7 \end{vmatrix} + 0 \begin{vmatrix} 2 & 3 \\ 3 & 2 \end{vmatrix} = 13 \times \left(-31 \right) = -403.$$

Hence

$$z = \dfrac{-403}{65} = -6.2.$$

Test yourself

Q7. Find the inverse of the matrix $\begin{pmatrix} 2 & -1 & 1 \\ 1 & 2 & 3 \\ 1 & 0 & -1 \end{pmatrix}$.

Q8. Use Cramer's rule to find the value of z in the system

$$\begin{aligned} 2x + 3y - z &= 8 \\ 3x + 4y - 2z &= 13 \\ x + 2y + 3z &= 0. \end{aligned}$$

Linear programming

A linear programming problem is one in which a linear expression (called the *objective function*) is optimised subject to a number of *linear constraints*. Three steps are needed to formulate such problems:

Step 1	Specify the variables used.
Step 2	Write down an expression for the objective function in terms of these variables.
Step 3	Find all of the constraints.

These steps are illustrated in the following example.

Worked example

I decide to extend my investment portfolio by spending no more than £2,500 on shares in companies A and B. The cost of each share is £5 and £10, respectively, and my financial advisor estimates that I can expect to make a profit of £0.40 and £0.65 on each share. Due to environmental concerns, I decide to buy at least twice as many shares in company B than A. Formulate this as a linear programming problem.

Solution

Step 1

In this problem I need to decide exactly how many shares of each type to buy, so these are the unknowns.

Let x = the numbers of shares in company A.

Let y = the number of shares in company B.

Step 2

I would like to maximise the estimated return from these shares. For each share of company A, I make a profit of £0.40 so if I buy x of these, the profit is $0.40x$. For company B the profit is $0.65y$, so the total return is $0.40x + 0.65y$, which is the objective function that is to be maximised.

Step 3

The price of each share is £5 and £10, respectively, so if I buy x shares for A and y shares for B the total cost is $5x + 10y$. The amount spent is limited to £2,500 so the first constraint is $5x + 10y \leq 2500$.

I am also restricted by the decision to buy at least twice as many shares in company B than A. For example, if I buy 25 shares in company A then I must buy at least 50 in company B. In general we have $y \geq 2x$.

Finally, note that because I am buying shares rather than selling them, the variables x and y are both non-negative, so we have the additional constraints $x \geq 0, y \geq 0$.

The linear programming problem is to maximise the objective function $0.40x + 0.65y$ subject to the constraints:

$$5x + 10y \leq 2500$$

$$y \geq 2x$$

$$x \geq 0, y \geq 0$$

Once a linear programming problem has been formulated, it needs to be solved. The *feasible region* consists of all possible combinations of variables that satisfy all of the constraints. For two variables, this region is usually a polygon. The optimal value of the objective function is attained at one of the corners of the region, so we simply evaluate the objective function at each corner in turn until we find the one that gives the highest (or lowest) value. The solution procedure can be summarised as follows:

Step 1	Sketch the feasible region.	
Step 2	Write down the coordinates of the corners of the region.	
Step 3	Evaluate the objective function at each corner and hence locate the optimal point.	

We illustrate the strategy by solving the previous worked example.

Worked example

Maximise the objective function $0.40x + 0.55y$ subject to the following constraints:

$$5x + 10y \leq 2500$$

$$y \geq 2x$$

$$x \geq 0, y \geq 0$$

Solution

Step 1

The last two constraints merely indicate that the region is confined to the top right-hand quadrant. This is illustrated below using the convention that the unwanted region has been shaded out.

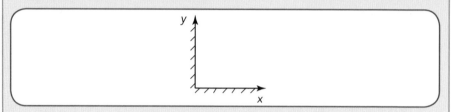

The points that satisfy the inequality $y \geq 2x$ are bounded by the line $y = 2x$, which passes through $(0,0)$, $(100, 200)$, $(200,400)$ and so on. To find which side of the line to cross out, we pick a "test point". Any point can be used, provided it does not lie on the line itself. For example, the test point $(300,200)$ fails to satisfy the inequality because the statement $200 \geq 2 \times 300$ is false. This point is on the side of the line that we want to remove, so the region below the line is shaded out:

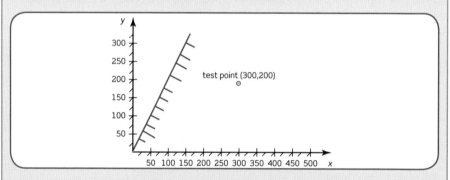

The points that satisfy the inequality $5x + 10y \leq 2500$ are bounded by the line $5x + 10y = 2500$. The simplest way of sketching this line is to find the intercepts.

The line crosses the y-axis when $x = 0$. Substituting this into $5x + 10y = 2500$ gives $10y = 2500$, so $y = 250$.

The line crosses the x-axis when $y = 0$. Substituting this into $5x + 10y = 2500$ gives $5x = 2500$, so $x = 500$.

The line is sketched overleaf. As a test point let us try $(200,100)$, which is below the line. This satisfies the inequality, because

$5 \times 200 + 10 \times 100 = 2000 \leq 2500$. The region below the line is therefore wanted, and so we shade out the region above this line:

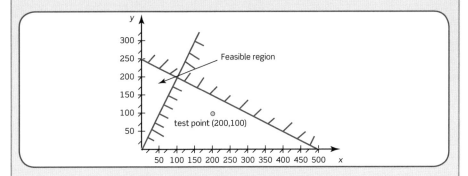

Step 2

The feasible region is a triangle with corners at (0,0), (100,200) and (0,250).

Step 3

The value of the objective function at each corner is as follows:

Point	Profit = 0.40x + 0.65y
(0,0)	0
(100,200)	£170
(0,250)	£162.50

I need to buy 100 shares of company A and 200 shares of company B to achieve a maximum profit of £170.

Test yourself

Q9. A company wants to organise a day out at the races for its 84 employees. A local taxi firm is able to provide transport in either a town-car or a people-carrier, which seat four and six passengers, respectively. It costs the company £120 to hire a town car and £180 for a people carrier. The taxi firm runs a fleet of 18 town cars and 8 people carriers. Advise the company on how many cars of each type it should order.

Chapter summary – pulling it all together

By the end of this chapter you should be able to:

	Confident ✓	Not confident?
Perform basic matrix operations including addition, subtraction and multiplication of two matrices		Revise pages 102–105
Use determinants and inverses to solve 2 × 2 systems		Revise pages 105–108
Use determinants and inverses to solve 3 × 3 systems		Revise pages 108–111
Formulate linear programming problems given in words		Revise pages 112–113
Solve linear programming problems graphically		Revise pages 113–115

Now try the assessment question at the start of the chapter using the answer guidelines below.

Answer guidelines

✴ Assessment question

(a) Use a matrix method to solve the following simultaneous equations:

$$4x + 3y = 900$$
$$5x + 7y = 1750.$$

Give your answers as fractions.

(b) A food supplier makes two different varieties of smoothie, "Exotic" and "Floridian", which it sells in 2-litre cartons. The main ingredients and profit made on each carton are as follows:

	Banana	Mango	Orange	Profit
Exotic	4	2	5	£2.25
Floridian	3	1	7	£2.00

The company has 900 bananas, 400 mangoes and 1,750 oranges to use, and wishes to arrange production to maximise total profit. It can sell all of the smoothies that it produces.

  (i)   Formulate this as a linear programming problem.

  (ii) Sketch the feasible region.

  (iii) Write down the exact coordinates of the corners of the region.

  (iv) Find the optimising production levels of each type of smoothie.

Approaching the question

- This question appears to be in two unrelated parts. But be aware that the answer to part (a) might be of use in part (b).

- The question asks you to solve the system of equations in part (a) using matrix methods. No credit would be given for using other approaches, such as elimination. However, you do still have a choice between Cramer's rule and using inverse matrices.

- The three-step strategy for problem formulation is described on page 112.

- The three-step strategy for the graphical solution is described on page 113.

- Don't forget to relate your final answer back to the original problem and check that it makes sense.

Method of solution

- Because the values of x and y are both required, it is marginally quicker to use inverses, although you are welcome to use Cramer's rule if you prefer because the method is not specified. You can check your final values by substituting them into both equations.

- Problem formulation is fairly straightforward. Don't forget to say what the letters x and y actually stand for. There are five constraints altogether including the two non-negativity constraints, which must be stated. There is an upper limit on each of the three types of fruit. You can read the table vertically to work out the total number of each type, and use the fact that each of these is less than or equal to the numbers available to write down each inequality.

- When sketching the feasible region it pays to work out the *x* and *y* intercepts of the three lines *before* you attempt to draw the diagram. You can then choose a sensible scale and range on each of the axes, making sure that all of the lines fit on the one diagram.

- You should find that the coordinates of the feasible region are easily read off the diagram, with one exception. In this case the coordinates are fractions, and it is not easy to read them off exactly from the diagram. Use your answer to part (a) to help you with this.

- This problem is known as an integer programming problem because we are only interested in producing whole numbers of cartons. If the answer is a fraction, you should just check out the points with integer coordinates that are inside the feasible region and near this corner. You then pick the one that maximises profit.

Companion website

Go to the companion website at **www.pearsoned.co.uk/econexpress** to find more revision support online for this topic area.

Notes

7 Descriptive statistics

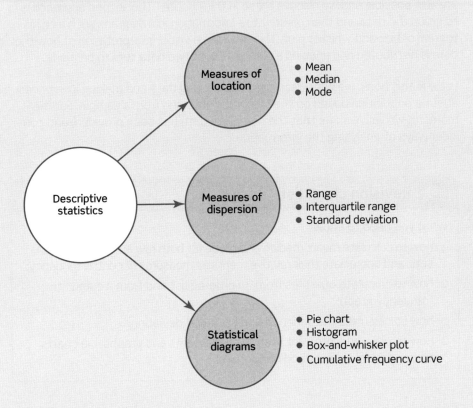

A printable version of this topic map is available from **www.pearsoned.co.uk/econexpress**

Introduction

Descriptive statistics provide us with a mechanism for summarising economic data and identifying its key features. If the data is merely provided in the form of numerical lists (whether on screen or on paper), it is virtually impossible for the human brain to make sense of it, to pick out any trends and to make a comparison between different data sets. However, data processing is crucial to many practical business situations, so it is important to be able to present the information in a fair and meaningful way.

There are two ways in which we can summarise data. Firstly, we can replace tens of thousands of numbers with just a few key numerical statistics, such as the mean and standard deviation, which help us to get a feel for where the data is centred and how spread out the data is around this centre. Other measures are also possible and we discuss these in this chapter. The second approach is to group the data and then present the information in a diagram, such as a histogram or box-and-whisker plot. This provides a visual interpretation of how the data is distributed and enables a comparison of two data sets to be made.

Later in this book, we consider ways of collecting data and making inferences about a population based on the statistics obtained from a sample. For the moment, we will assume that the complete data has been provided, and consider ways of analysing the information.

 Revision checklist

What you need to know:

- ❑ how to calculate mean, median and mode for both raw and grouped data sets, and appreciate their relative merits as measures of central tendency;
- ❑ how to calculate quartiles from an ordered list and from a cumulative frequency graph;
- ❑ how to calculate the variance and standard deviation;
- ❑ how to draw and interpret statistical diagrams and graphs: pie charts, box-and-whisker plots and histograms.

✳ Assessment advice

- ● Make sure that you know the pros and cons of using the mean, median and mode, as well as how to calculate each one.

- Remember that bar charts must not be used for unequal class widths. Use histograms, where the heights of the bars are frequency density instead of frequency.
- Be aware that, when dealing with grouped data, you use the upper class boundaries for drawing cumulative frequency graphs, but use the midpoints when calculating mean and standard deviation.
- Be prepared to comment and interpret your results and diagrams *in context*.
- There are so many ways of summarising data because there is no perfect method that suits every situation. The choice depends on the type of data, the target audience, the purpose of providing the data and so on. Try to think about possible reasons for choosing any particular statistical diagram over another.
- Don't just use the mean or median to compare data sets. Comment on other features such as the spread and skewness, as well as highlighting other aspects from a statistical diagram.
- Familiarise yourself with the statistical features of your calculator. Although it is important that you understand how the various statistics are worked out, in an examination you can save valuable time by using your machine efficiently.
- There are two versions of standard deviation depending on whether you divide by n or $n-1$. These are distinguished on a calculator by labelling them σ_n and σ_{n-1}, respectively. You divide by n when you want to find the standard deviation of the available data set (or believe that you have the complete data set). If you only have a sample of the data, and want to estimate the standard deviation of the complete set from which this sample is taken, then you divide by $n-1$. In this chapter we assume that the complete data set is provided and so use σ_n. Sampling is discussed fully in Chapter 9.

✳ Assessment question

Could you answer this question? Guidelines on answering the question are presented at the end of this chapter.

(a) Discuss the relative merits of using the mean and median as measures of central tendency.

(b) Investment company A manages 200 separate £2,000 investments in a variety of different portfolios, and the profit (or loss) made on each one is shown in Table 7.1. Estimate the median and quartiles of this data set, and hence draw a box-and-whisker plot.

Table 7.1

Profit (in £100s)	−5 ≤ p < 0	0 ≤ p < 5	5 ≤ p < 10	10 ≤ p < 15	15 ≤ p < 20
Frequency	33	47	58	37	25

Figure 7.1 shows three more box plots for rival firms B, C and D.

(c) Compare the returns made from investments in companies A and B.

(d) Upon retirement, Maud decides that she is going to invest all of her life savings in either company A or company B. What advice can you give her? Give reasons for your answer.

(e) Which of companies A or B would you choose to invest in, if you wanted to select one of them to outperform (i) C or (ii) D? Give reasons for your answer.

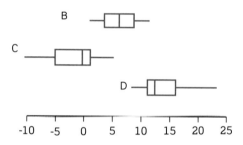

Figure 7.1

Measures of location

Three different types of average can be calculated to provide an idea of where the "centre" of a distribution might lie.

Key definition

The **mean**, $\bar{x}$, is the sum of the values in a data set divided by the number of values.

In symbols we write

$$\bar{x} = \frac{1}{n}\Sigma x,$$

where the Greek letter sigma, Σ, is an instruction for us to add numbers together. For example, the mean of the six numbers 3, 2, 7, 10, 60, 2 is

$$\bar{x} = \frac{3 + 2 + 7 + 10 + 60 + 2}{6} = \frac{84}{6} = 14.$$

This is what most people refer to when they use the word "average". It has the advantage that a simple mathematical process can be applied to the data as it stands, and that every number in the data set makes a contribution. However, this sensitivity is also a drawback. The mean is distorted by one or two extreme values or outliers. In this example the presence of the number 60 has resulted in a mean of 14, which cannot be regarded as a true representation of the data. The mean plays a crucial role in inferential statistics, and for this reason it is the mean that is the most widely used average in advanced statistics.

Key definition

The **median** is the middle value when the data is arranged in numerical order.

To find the median of the data set above, first put the numbers in order: 2, 2, 3, 7, 10, 60.

There are two numbers in the middle, 3 and 7, so the median is halfway between them:

$$\text{Median} = \frac{1}{2}(3 + 7) = 5.$$

In general, the median of an ordered list of n numbers is the

$$\frac{1}{2}(n + 1)\text{th}$$

item. If n is odd, there is just one middle value (e.g. when $n = 13$ the median is the

$$\frac{1}{2}(13 + 1)\text{th} = 7\text{th item,}$$

whereas when n is even there are two middle values (e.g. in the above example, $n = 6$ so the median is the

123

$$\frac{1}{2}(6 + 1)\text{th} = 3.5\text{th item,}$$

which we interpret as being halfway between the 3rd and 4th items).

The median is relatively insensitive to the actual values in a data set (replacing the numbers 10 and 60 in the previous example with, say, 20 and 160 would have no effect on the median) but this does have the advantage of being unaffected by extreme values. It also gives the true "central" location. On the downside, the list has to be ordered first and, as we shall see later, it may be necessary to estimate its value using a graph when the data is grouped.

Key definition

The **mode** is the most frequent item in a data set.

For the previous data set the mode is 2 because this number appears twice in the list and the other numbers occur only once. The mode is very simple to work out. However, the value it gives may not be a central value (2 is actually the lowest item in the previous data set), so it is not really fit for purpose. Also, it is possible for there to be two items of the highest frequency (a bimodal distribution) or for every item to occur with the same frequency (in which case there isn't a mode at all).

Test yourself

Q1. Find the mean, median and mode of this data set. Which of these averages provides the best measure of central tendency? Give reasons for your answer.

3, 6, 7, 21, 4, 5, 3, 7

Measures of dispersion

In addition to finding the central tendency of a distribution, it is important to know how the data is dispersed around this value. The median of the data sets below are both 5, but the way that the numbers are distributed is very different:

Data set A: 3, 3, 4, 4, 4, 5, 7, 8, 9, 11, 13

Data set B: 0, 3, 4, 4, 4, 5, 5, 6, 6, 6, 7, 10

Key definition

The **range** is the difference between the largest and smallest numbers in a data set.

This statistic is easy to work out and interpret but, as in the case of the mean, it can give a false impression if there are extreme values. It also fails to identify how the data is spread within these extremes; the range is the same for data sets A and B (both 10), even though they have quite different distributions.

A more subtle alternative is to use the interquartile range, which measures the spread of the middle 50% of the data set.

Key definitions

The **lower** (and **upper**) **quartiles** are located a quarter (and three-quarters) of the way through a data set. The **interquartile range** (IQR) is the difference between these quartiles.

One way of finding the quartiles is to split a data set in half and then find the median of each half separately. Data set A has an odd number of items. We take out the middle number (which is the median, 5) so that it splits into two equal halves.

The lower half of set A – 3, 3, 4, 4, 4 – has a median of 4, so this is the lower quartile.

The upper half of set A – 7, 8, 9, 11, 13 – has a median of 9, so this is the upper quartile.

Hence IQR = 9 – 4 = 5.

Data set B has an even number of items so splits more easily into two sets of 6. The same calculations give an IQR of 6 – 4 = 2, which is much smaller than the IQR in set A. This reflects the fact that the bulk of the data is further away from the median in set A than in B. The IQR provides a reasonable way of comparing data sets, and knowledge of the quartiles themselves gives us an indication of how the numbers are distributed within the data set. The disadvantages are the same as for the median: the calculation of the quartiles requires an ordered list of numbers, and it is sometimes necessary to estimate quartiles graphically.

In fact, all five numbers – smallest, lower quartile, median, upper quartile and largest – can be displayed on a *box-and-whisker plot* (sometimes just called a *box plot*), as shown in Figure 7.2.

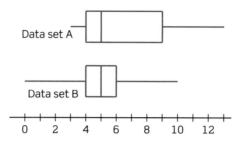

Figure 7.2

If this is the only information available then you can immediately read off the quartiles and extreme values from the scale provided. It also reveals another characteristic of the data sets, namely the *skewness*. The box plot for set B is *symmetrical*, with the median exactly in the middle of the box and the whiskers perfectly balanced. For A it appears as if the whole diagram has stretched out to the right (in the direction of the positive *x*-axis). We describe this by saying that the distribution is *positively skewed*.

Key definition

The **variance** measures the spread of data about the mean:

$$\text{Variance} = \frac{1}{n}\sum(x - \bar{x})^2 = \frac{1}{n}\sum x^2 - \bar{x}^2.$$

Notice that there are two different formulae that you can use for calculating the variance. They both give the same numerical value. The first is the actual definition. The numbers, $(x - \bar{x})^2$, give the square of the distance of each number in the data set away from the mean. The average of these numbers is then found. The second formula is easier to apply, so this is the version that we use in calculations. It can be remembered as "the mean of the squares minus the square of the mean". For data set A:

$$\text{Mean} = \frac{3 + 3 + 4 + 4 + 4 + 5 + 7 + 8 + 9 + 11 + 13}{11} = \frac{71}{11}$$

Mean of the squares =
$$\frac{3^2 + 3^2 + 4^2 + 4^2 + 4^2 + 5^2 + 7^2 + 8^2 + 9^2 + 11^2 + 13^2}{11} = \frac{575}{11}$$

$$\text{Variance} = \frac{575}{11} - \left(\frac{71}{11}\right)^2 = \frac{1284}{121} = 10.6$$

It is important to notice that, unlike all of the other statistics considered so far, the variance is not given in the same units as the original data. If monetary data is available in US dollars then the variance would be measured in (US dollars)^2, which is meaningless. We avoid this difficulty by calculating the *standard deviation* instead. This is defined as the square root of the variance.

For data set A the standard deviation is

$$\sqrt{\frac{1284}{121}} = 3.26$$

This is the measure of spread used in advanced statistics. Most calculators have statistical menus that allow you to just enter the data and press the appropriate button. Excel has similar features so the evaluation of the standard deviation is quite easy. The standard deviation provides an excellent way of comparing data sets (provided the means are not too dissimilar), although it is not so easy to interpret individual values (see Chapter 8 for the case when the data is normally distributed).

Test yourself.

Q2. (a) Find the mean and standard deviation of data set B, given earlier.

(b) Data set C (not given) has a mean and standard deviation of 20 and 4, respectively. Use this information to describe any differences and similarities between these three sets of data.

Statistical diagrams

Data can often be divided into non-overlapping categories. Pie charts provide a simple, but eye-catching, way of demonstrating the relative proportion of each category by allocating a sector (slice of pie) to each one.

Worked example

Draw a pie chart for the data in the following table, which shows the number of students (rounded to the nearest five) awarded particular degree classifications at UK higher education institutions in 2010–11.

First	Upper second	Lower second	Third	Unclassified	Total
53,215	166,100	99,210	24,825	25,540	368,890

Source: Higher Education Statistics Agency, **www.hesa.ac.uk**

Solution

The percentage of students awarded first-class degrees was

$$\frac{53215}{368890} \times 100 = 14\%.$$

To work out the angle of the corresponding sector on a pie chart, multiply 360 by 0.14 to get 52°. The complete diagram is shown in Figure 7.3.

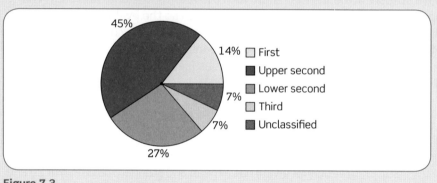

Figure 7.3

Pie charts are only really useful when there are just a few categories. If not, the picture becomes too crowded, although it does have the advantage that it can be used to display non-numerical data.

In practice, we often need to illustrate numerical data that is supplied to us in groups (or classes). People are often reluctant to provide personal information such as their precise age or salary, but are more willing to tick a box that covers a range of values. The blunt question "What is your annual salary?" is more likely to be answered honestly if people are presented with a range of tick boxes such as:

Under £10,000 ☐

Between £10,000 and £20,000 ☐

possibly finishing with an open-ended option such as:

Over £75,000 ☐

There would, of course, need to be an instruction about which box to tick in the unlikely event that someone earns exactly £10,000.

Even if the data is not supplied in groups, it is often convenient to arrange it into groups to make it easier to analyse. The most common way of representing such information diagrammatically is to use a bar chart, where the height of each bar represents frequency. However, if the groups are of unequal width this is misleading. As an example, consider the data in Table 7.2, which shows the annual salary of 250 employees of a medium-sized firm.

The fact that the last group has the second-highest frequency may be more to do with the fact that this group covers the widest range of salary rather than any innate "popularity" of the data. On the other hand, the fourth group contains a surprisingly large number of people when you take into account the fact that the width of this group is relatively small. To adjust for this, and to create a level playing field, we plot *frequency density* on the vertical axis instead of frequency, where

$$\text{frequency density} = \frac{\text{frequency}}{\text{class width}}.$$

The corresponding bar chart is called a *histogram*. Frequencies are then represented by the *area* of each bar rather than the height. The calculations are shown in the last column of Table 7.2, and the histogram itself is displayed in Figure 7.4. The modal class (the group with the highest bar on a histogram) is 35–45, so a sensible estimate of the mode is 40.

One disadvantage of using grouped data is that it is no longer possible to work out the exact values of statistics such as the median and standard deviation. If we assume that the data is spread evenly within each class, then estimates can be found as demonstrated in the following example.

Table 7.2

Annual salary (£1,000s)	Number of employees (frequency)	Frequency density
0–10	15	15/10 = 1.5
10–20	25	25/10 = 2.5
20–30	42	42/10 = 4.2
30–35	31	31/5 = 6.2
35–45	77	77/10 = 7.7
45–60	60	60/15 = 4

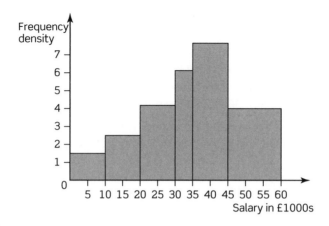

Figure 7.4

Worked example

For the data provided in Table 7.2:

(a) estimate the mean and standard deviation;

(b) use a cumulative frequency graph to estimate the interquartile range and draw an approximate box plot.

Solution

(a) The first row of the table shows that there are 15 people earning somewhere between £0 and £10,000, so it seems reasonable to take the mid-point of this class as an estimate of the salary of each of these employees. The contribution of these 15 people to the total sum needed for the calculation of the mean is therefore roughly $5000 \times 15 = 75000$. For the standard deviation, we need the sum of the squares, so the contribution from the first group to this total is $5000^2 \times 15 = 375,000,000$. Columns 3, 4 and 5 in Table 7.3 show the complete set of calculations.

To avoid writing down lots of zeros we have chosen to work with the numbers given in the first column. The mean and standard deviation are then measured in £1,000s and are found from:

$$\bar{x} = \frac{1}{n}\sum fx = \frac{8737.5}{250} = 34.95;$$

standard deviation =

$$\sqrt{\frac{1}{n}\sum fx^2 - \bar{x}^2} = \sqrt{\frac{353568.75}{250} - 34.95^2} = 13.88,$$

where f and x denote the frequency and mid-point of each group.

Table 7.3

Annual salary	Frequency (f)	Mid-point (x)	fx	fx²	Upper class boundaries	Cumulative frequency
0–10	15	5	75	375	10	15
10–20	25	15	375	5,625	20	40
20–30	42	25	1,050	26,250	30	82
30–35	31	32.5	1,007.5	32,743.75	35	113
35–45	77	40	3,080	123,200	45	190
45–60	60	52.5	3,150	165,375	60	250
Total	250		8,737.5	353,568.75		

(b) The last two columns in Table 7.3 show the upper class boundaries of each group (the highest salary in each class) together with the cumulative frequency (the running total). For example, in the third row of the table we see that there are 82 people, in total, earning anything up to £30,000. A graph of cumulative frequency plotted against the upper class boundaries is shown in Figure 7.5.

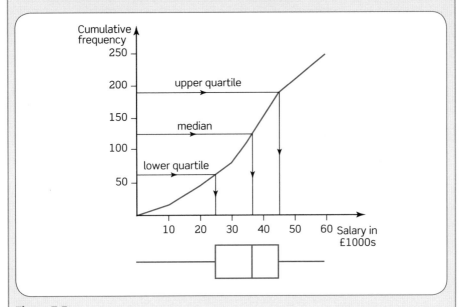

Figure 7.5

The median is approximately 37 and is worked out by going halfway up the vertical axis, drawing a horizontal line across to the graph and then reading off the median on the horizontal axis. The quartiles are approximately 25 and 45 and are worked out in the same way, by going one-quarter and three-quarters of the way up, respectively. The box plot is drawn conveniently underneath the graph. By joining the points with straight lines, we are making the assumption that the individual data points are spread uniformly within each group. An alternative would be to join the points by a smooth curve. In this case the spread of data within each group is no longer uniform, but is influenced by the data in the groups on either side.

Notice that both the histogram and box plot show visually that the data is skewed negatively. The numerical values of the mean, median and mode are 35, 37 and 40 with mean < median < mode.

For a positively skewed distribution, this ordering is reversed.

Test yourself

Q3. The annual salaries (in thousands of pounds) of a rival firm are listed in Table 7.4.

Table 7.4

Salary (in £1,000s)	0-10	10-20	20-25	25-30	30-40	40-60
Frequency	10	33	40	42	29	22

(a) Draw a histogram.

(b) Find the mean and standard deviation.

(c) Use your answers to parts (a) and (b) to compare the distribution of salaries between this firm and the one considered in the previous worked example.

Chapter summary – pulling it all together

By the end of this chapter you should be able to:

	Confident ✓	Not confident?
Calculate the mean, median and mode of a list of numbers		Revise pages 122–124
Know the advantages and disadvantages of each average		Revise pages 122–124
Calculate the interquartile range and draw a box plot of a list of numbers		Revise pages 125–126
Calculate the standard deviation of a list of numbers		Revise pages 126–127
Draw pie charts and histograms		Revise pages 127–130
Estimate the mean and standard deviation of grouped data		Revise pages 130–131
Use a cumulative frequency graph to estimate the median and quartiles of grouped data		Revise pages 131–132

Now try the assessment question at the start of the chapter using the answer guidelines below.

Answer guidelines

✳ Assessment question

(a) Discuss the relative merits of using the mean and median as measures of central tendency.

(b) Investment company A manages 200 separate £2,000 investments, in a variety of different portfolios, and the profit (or loss) made on each is shown in Table 7.1. Estimate the median and quartiles of this data set and hence draw a box-and-whisker plot.

Figure 7.1 shows three more box plots for rival firms B, C and D.

(c) Compare the returns made from investments in companies A and B.

(d) Upon retirement, Maud decides that she is going to invest all of her life savings in either company A or company B. What advice can you give her? Give reasons for your answer.

(e) Which of companies A or B would you choose to invest in if you wanted to select one of them to outperform (i) C or (ii) D? Give reasons for your answer.

Approaching the question

- This question is in five parts. You need the answer to the second part in order to complete the rest of the question.

- Decide at the beginning exactly what individual steps are needed to tackle each part.

- Part (a) is very general. It is merely asking you to list the pros and cons of the mean and median. This is a standard question testing to see if you appreciate (and have learnt) the strengths and weaknesses of statistical measures.

- Part (b) is the only technical part. You need to calculate the quartiles of a grouped data set. What methods do you know for doing this?

- The last three parts test your ability to interpret statistical diagrams. Make sure that you know exactly what a box plot represents and try to give your comments in context.

Method of solution

- In part (b) you must first work out the quartiles. There are two ways of doing this:

  - Draw a cumulative frequency graph. Remember to plot the upper class boundaries on the horizontal axis and cumulative frequencies on the vertical axis. The median is found by going halfway up the vertical axis, drawing a horizontal line across to the graph and then reading the answer off the horizontal axis. The quartiles are worked out similarly.

  - It is possible to find the median by first working out in which class it lies, and then interpolating to estimate where the median will be. In this case, the median is the 100th item. The first two groups total 80 so the median is the 20th number out of the 58 numbers in the third group. Therefore, we take the median to be 20/58th of the way from 5 to 10.

- A graphics calculator can also be used to find the quartiles (and draw a box-and-whisker plot).
- Part (c) asks for a comparison of two data sets by inspection of their box plots. It helps if you draw both box plots underneath each other on the same diagram. Don't forget to mention:
  - the median, which allows you to compare the average profit;
  - the interquartile range, which allows you to compare the spread;
  - the shape of the box plot, which allows you to compare skewness.
- In part (d) you need to offer advice to Maud. She is clearly looking for a safe investment and cannot afford to pick an option in which she might lose money. A company offering a low spread and high average is required.
- By contrast, in part (e) (i) you must find a firm that has a reasonable chance of producing a better return than C. This cannot be guaranteed and inevitably carries a degree of risk. Likewise for (e) (ii).

Companion website

Go to the companion website at **www.pearsoned.co.uk/econexpress** to find more revision support online for this topic area.

Notes

8 Probability distributions

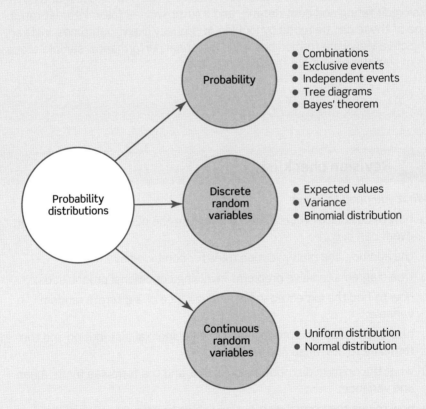

- Probability
  - Combinations
  - Exclusive events
  - Independent events
  - Tree diagrams
  - Bayes' theorem

- Discrete random variables
  - Expected values
  - Variance
  - Binomial distribution

- Continuous random variables
  - Uniform distribution
  - Normal distribution

A printable version of this topic map is available from **www.pearsoned.co.uk/econexpress**

Introduction

In this chapter we consider uncertainty. A firm will know what the sales figures were for the previous year but would like to predict what will happen in the future. It cannot know what trading conditions are going to be but would like to work out the chances of various options so that an informed choice can be made. Probability provides a numerical measure of uncertainty. It is a number between 0 and 1; the extreme values corresponding to events that are impossible or certain to occur, respectively.

The theory of probability was originally developed for gambling. The probability of obtaining a four when a single dice is rolled is 1/6 because a four is just one of six equally likely outcomes. However, today probabilities are attached to events that cannot be assessed by counting the number of equally likely outcomes. It is useful to be able to estimate the probabilities of events such as the rise in the cost of fuel and raw materials, the downgrading of a country's credit rating and debt default, and a future rise or fall in interest rates. None of these can be found by looking at "equally likely" outcomes. Instead, subjective views are formed based on historical performance, sample statistics or sometimes just old-fashioned intuition.

 ## Revision checklist

What you need to know:

- ❑ how to calculate probabilities by counting the number of ways that an event can occur;
- ❑ the addition and multiplication rules for combined events;
- ❑ tree diagrams to solve problems involving conditional probabilities;
- ❑ how to find the expected value and variance of a discrete random variable;
- ❑ how to calculate the probabilities of the binomial distribution and the formulae for its mean and variance;
- ❑ what the uniform distribution looks like, and the formulae for its mean and variance;
- ❑ how to use the normal distribution tables to calculate probabilities.

✳ Assessment advice

- It is useful to understand where the ^nC_r formula comes from so that you recognise situations where it can be used.
- Make sure that you know the difference between exclusive and independent events, and what the consequences of these are.
- Although not compulsory, drawing a tree diagram sometimes helps to organise your thoughts.
- Learn the formulae for the calculation of the mean and variance of general discrete random variables.
- Learn the specific formulae for the mean and variance of the binomial and uniform distributions.
- The binomial distribution is only valid when certain conditions hold. You need to learn these and be prepared to comment critically on whether these are likely to be satisfied in any particular situation.
- Practise using the normal distribution tables (or your calculator) to work out probabilities. This skill is used repeatedly in the next two chapters, so it is important that you can use the tables (or your calculator) quickly and accurately.

✳ Assessment question

Could you answer this question? Guidelines on answering the question are presented at the end of this chapter.

Marks awarded on a course are known to be normally distributed with mean, μ, and standard deviation, σ. Based on these raw marks, degrees are classified as follows:

Marks	Degree classification
$x < 35$	Fail
$35 \leq x < 45$	Third
$45 \leq x < 56$	Lower second
$56 \leq x < 73$	Upper second
$x \geq 73$	First

(a) If 8% of candidates are awarded first class degrees, show that
$1.406\sigma + \mu = 73$.

If 5% fail the course, write down a second equation and hence determine
the values of μ and σ, correct to two decimal places.

(b) Show that 40.4% of candidates are awarded upper-second class
degrees.

(c) Use the binomial distribution to calculate the probability that, in a group
of 10 students, exactly half have upper-second class degrees.

(d) Comment on the validity of using the binomial model in part (c).

Probability

Key definition

If the outcomes are equally likely then the **probability of an event, E,** is
given by

$$P(E) = \frac{\text{number of outcomes in which the event occurs}}{\text{total number of possible outcomes}}$$

This definition is easy to use if the number of outcomes is readily available.
The table below shows the degree courses taken by 200 students in a hall of
residence.

	Science	Business	Languages	Arts	Total
Men	47	25	8	27	107
Women	25	38	10	20	93
Total	72	63	18	47	200

If a person is chosen at random from this hall of residence the probabilities
that this person is

• a woman is

$$\frac{93}{200} = 0.465;$$

- studying languages is

$$\frac{18}{200} = 0.09;$$

- a man studying business is

$$\frac{25}{200} = 0.125.$$

If the numbers of equally likely outcomes are not known, it is sometimes possible to work them out without going to the trouble of listing each one, as the following example demonstrates.

Worked example

A jury in a criminal court of law consists of 12 people. These are chosen at random from a group of 9 women and 6 men. What is the probability of picking a jury of 8 women and 4 men?

Solution

Before we consider this problem it is useful to introduce a piece of notation. We write $n!$ (read n factorial) as an abbreviation for $n \times (n - 1) \times (n - 2) \times \ldots \times 3 \times 2 \times 1$. This gives the number of ways in which n objects can be arranged in a line. For example, if the letters A, B and C are arranged in the spaces

there are three choices (A, B, or C) for the first space. Suppose the letter B is placed in this:

| B | | |

There are then two choices (in this case A or C) to put in the second space. Of course once this has been done, the remaining letter must go in the last space, so there is only one choice here. The total number of ways of arranging the three letters is $3 \times 2 \times 1 = 3!$.

For the jury problem, imagine you are the clerk responsible for choosing the 12 people from the group of 15. There are 15 possibilities for the first person. Once they have been picked, there are 14 left to choose from for the second person and so on. When you come to pick the last person there will be 4 to choose. The total number of ways is therefore given by

$$15 \times 14 \times 13 \times 12 \times \ldots \times 4$$

$$= \frac{15 \times 14 \times 13 \times 12 \times \ldots \times 4 \times (3 \times 2 \times 1)}{(3 \times 2 \times 1)}$$

$$= \frac{15!}{3!}.$$

In fact, the number of possible juries is not as large as this: many of these options lead to juries comprising the same people picked in a different order. As we have just seen, there are 12! ways of shuffling 12 objects around so the total number of different juries is

$$\frac{15!}{12!3!},$$

which is written as $^{15}C_{12}$.

The number of ways of choosing r objects from n objects (when the ordering doesn't matter) is

$$^{n}C_{r} = \frac{n!}{r!(n-r)}.$$

Using the $^{n}C_{r}$ button on a calculator, $^{15}C_{12} = 455$.

To find the probability, we need to find out how many of the 455 potential juries consist of 8 women and 4 men. The clerk needs to pick 8 women from the 9 available and 4 men from the 6 available. The number of ways of doing this is $^{9}C_{8} \times ^{6}C_{4} = 9 \times 15 = 135$. The probability of selecting such a jury at random is then

$$\frac{135}{455} = \frac{27}{91}$$

which is approximately 30%.

Test yourself

Q1. The students' union committee consists of 24 students. These are chosen at random from a group of 16 men and 20 women. What is the probability of picking a committee consisting of 14 men and 10 women?

Key definitions

Events A and B are (mutually) **exclusive** if they cannot occur at the same time (so there is no overlap between these events). For exclusive events, $P(A \text{ or } B) = P(A) + P(B)$. This is called the **addition law of probability**.

Events A and B are **independent** if the occurrence of one of these does not affect the occurrence of the other. For independent events, $P(A \text{ and } B) = P(A) \times P(B)$. This is called the **multiplication law of probability**.

Worked example

A company manufactures three unrelated products, A, B and C. The probability that one of these items is faulty is 0.05, 0.1 and 0.02, respectively. If one item of each type is supplied, what is the probability that

(a) none are faulty?

(b) exactly two are faulty?

Solution

If the probability that an item of type A is faulty is 0.05, then the probability that it is not faulty must be $1 - 0.05 = 0.95$. In the same way, the probability that an item of type B and C is not faulty is 0.9 and 0.98, respectively.

(a) P(A is not faulty and B is not faulty and C is not faulty)
$= 0.95 \times 0.9 \times 0.98 = 0.8379$ (multiplication rule).

(b) This situation could arise in one of three ways:

- (A faulty and B faulty and C not faulty);
- (A faulty and B not faulty and C faulty); or
- (A not faulty and B faulty and C faulty).

These combinations are mutually exclusive, so we can use the addition rule for each combination and so get $(0.05 \times 0.1 \times 0.98) + (0.05 \times 0.9 \times 0.02) + (0.95 \times 0.1 \times 0.02) = 0.0077$.

Test yourself

Q2. The probability that a parcel is delivered on time by companies A and B is 0.9 and 0.8, respectively.

(a) If company A and company B deliver one parcel each, what is the probability that

(i) both arrive on time?

(ii) at least one arrives on time?

(b) If company A delivers three parcels and company B delivers four parcels, what is the probability that all seven parcels arrive on time?

State any assumptions that you have made to obtain your answers. Are these assumptions likely to be justified in practice?

An obvious question to ask is: what happens when the events are *not* mutually exclusive or *not* independent? The first is dealt with easily.

The addition rule generalises to give $P(A \text{ or } B) = P(A) + P(B) - P(A \text{ and } B)$ because if the events overlap, then we need to subtract the probability of this occurring to prevent the overlap being counted twice.

If events A and B are not independent, we can still calculate the probability of the combined event "A and B" by multiplying two probabilities together, although this time one of them is a *conditional probability*. As an example, suppose there is a 0.2 chance of it raining one day (R). If it rains, then there is a 0.7 chance that I will carry an umbrella (U), whereas on dry days (D) this falls to 0.05. The number 0.7 is the conditional probability that I carry an umbrella given that it rains. This is written as $P(U|R)$. Similarly, we have $P(U|D) = 0.05$. The probability that it is a rainy day and I have an umbrella is worked out from $P(R \text{ and } U) = P(U|R) \times P(R) = 0.7 \times 0.2 = 0.14$.

Worked example

For the above events, find:

(a) the probability that I carry an umbrella;

(b) the conditional probability that it is raining given that I carry an umbrella.

Solution

The easiest way of organising the information is to use a tree diagram:

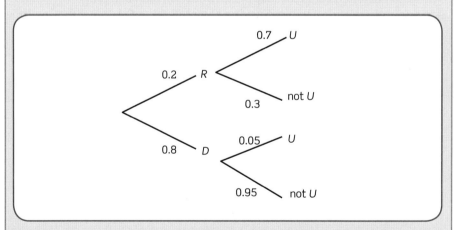

(a) The numbers on the second set of branches show the conditional probabilities. There are two routes on the diagram that lead to the event that I carry an umbrella. The probability of each route can be found by multiplying the probabilities and, because the routes are exclusive, we can add these two products together:
$P(U) = P(U|R) \times P(R) + P(U|D) \times P(D) = 0.7 \times 0.2 + 0.05 \times 0.8$
$= 0.18$.

(b) The rule for multiplying probabilities, $P(R \text{ and } U) = P(R|U) \times P(U)$, can be rearranged as

$$P(R|U) = \frac{P(R \text{ and } U)}{P(U)}.$$

We already know that $P(R \text{ and } U) = 0.14$ and from part (a) that $P(U) = 0.18$ so

$$P(R|U) = \frac{0.14}{0.18} = \frac{7}{9}.$$

The conditional probability in part (b) is both interesting and controversial, because it seems to imply that the state of the weather is somehow dependent on whether I happen to have an umbrella with me. In symbols, the result can be expressed as

$$P(R|U) = \frac{P(R \text{ and } U)}{P(U)} = \frac{P(U \text{ and } R)}{P(U)} = \frac{P(U|R) \times P(R)}{P(U|R) \times P(R) + P(U|D) \times P(D)}$$

and is known as *Bayes' theorem*.

Test yourself

Q3. The probability that I am happy at Sophie's party is 0.6. If I am happy the probability that I get drunk is 0.1. If I am unhappy this probability rises to 0.7.

(a) What is the probability that I get drunk at Sophie's party?

(b) Given that I get drunk, what is the probability that I am happy?

Discrete random variables

Key definitions

A **discrete random variable**, X, takes values x_i, with probability, p_i. The **expected value** of X is given by $E(X) = \sum x_i p_i$.

This definition is understood most easily using an example. The table lists the scores and the associated probabilities when a single die is thrown.

x_i	1	2	3	4	5	6
p_i	1/6	1/6	1/6	1/6	1/6	1/6

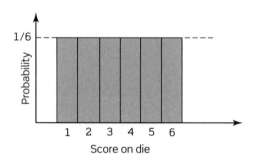

Figure 8.1

If a random variable, X, denotes the scores, then X takes six possible values and, because these are all equally likely, the probabilities are the same in each case. The probability distribution is shown in Figure 8.1.

The expected value of X is worked out by multiplying each value by its corresponding probability:

$$E(X) = \sum x_i p_i = 1 \times \frac{1}{6} + 2 \times \frac{1}{6} + 3 \times \frac{1}{6} + 4 \times \frac{1}{6} + 5 \times \frac{1}{6} + 6 \times \frac{1}{6} = 3.5.$$

Be careful when interpreting this value. It does not mean that we expect to get a score of 3.5 when we roll a die (which is, of course, impossible). However, it tells us that on average the score will be 3.5. In other words, if we were to actually conduct the experiment and roll the die lots and lots of times, the mean of the observed scores would get ever closer to 3.5. The expected value gives a theoretical mean for a model of a fair die. We sometimes write this using the Greek letter μ (mu) to distinguish it from the mean of an actual data set, which we write as $\bar{x}$.

Test yourself

Q4. Market stallholders A and B sell ice-cream and umbrellas, respectively. Potential profit for a day's trading is heavily dependent on the weather, as shown in the table overleaf, which gives the probabilities of a sunny, cloudy or wet day tomorrow. Which stall is expected to produce the higher profit tomorrow?

	Sunny	Cloudy	Wet
Probability	0.1	0.3	0.6
A	£240	£130	£50
B	£20	£80	£150

It is possible to calculate a theoretical variance as well. By analogy with the formula for the variance of a data set in Chapter 7, we have

$$Var(X) = \sum x_i^2 p_i - \mu^2.$$

The square root of the variance is the standard deviation. This is written as the Greek lower-case letter σ (sigma).

Worked example

The probability that I am late for work is 0.2. If X denotes the number of days on which I am late in a period of a week, calculate the mean and variance of X.

Solution

The probability that I am not late for work on any one day is $1 - 0.2 = 0.8$.

In order to solve this problem it is necessary to make several assumptions:

- I work for five days a week.
- The probability that I am late is constant throughout the week.
- My lateness for work on one day is independent of lateness on any other day.

The last two assumptions may not be realistic in practice. Road traffic on Mondays and Fridays tends to be lighter than on other days, so if I travel to work by car the probability of being late might be higher midweek. Also, if I find that I am late for work on any one day then I might make a real effort not to be late on the next day, so independence might not hold. Despite these reservations, we will assume that the model is reasonable.

The probability that I am not late all week is
$0.8 \times 0.8 \times 0.8 \times 0.8 \times 0.8 = (0.8)^5 = 0.32768$ using the multiplication rule for independent events.

If I am late just once, then I am on time four days so the probability is 0.2×0.8^4. However, there are actually five ways that this can occur depending on which of the five days is my late day, so the overall probability is $5 \times 0.2 \times 0.8^4 = 0.4096$, using the addition rule for exclusive events.

If I am late twice, then I must have been on time three times with a probability of $0.2^2 \times 0.8^3$. There are several ways in which this can be done and it is worth pausing to think how we could find the number of ways. The two "lates" and three "on times" need to be put into the weekly diary:

Monday	Tuesday	Wednesday	Thursday	Friday

You can begin by choosing which two out of the five days are going to be the late days. The number of ways of doing this is $^5C_2 = 10$. Once these have been selected the remaining three days are automatically filled in with on-time days, so no further choices are made. The total probability of being late two days out of five is then $^5C_2 \times 0.2^2 \times 0.8^3 = 0.2048$.

The remaining options can be worked out in the same way:

- $P(\text{late 3 days}) = {}^5C_3 \times 0.2^3 \times 0.8^2 = 0.0512;$
- $P(\text{late 4 days}) = {}^5C_4 \times 0.2^4 \times 0.8 = 0.0064;$
- $P(\text{late 5 days}) = {}^5C_5 \times 0.2^5 = 0.00032.$

The table below shows the values and probabilities of the random variable X. As a check, notice that these probabilities add up to 1.

x_i	0	1	2	3	4	5
p_i	0.32768	0.4096	0.2048	0.0512	0.0064	0.00032

The probability distribution is shown in Figure 8.2.

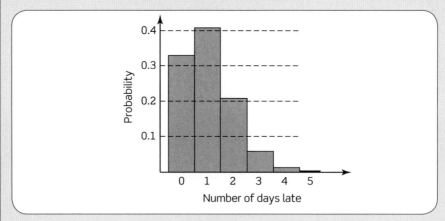

Figure 8.2

The mean and variance of X are calculated as follows:

$$\mu = \sum x_i p_i = 0 \times 0.32768 + 1 \times 0.4096 + 2 \times 0.2048$$

$$+ 3 \times 0.0512 + 4 \times 0.0064 + 5 \times 0.00032 = 1$$

$$\sigma^2 = \sum x_i^2 p - \mu^2$$

$$= 0^2 \times 0.32768 + 1^2 \times 0.4096 + 2^2 \times 0.2048 + 3^2 \times 0.0512$$

$$+ 4^2 \times 0.0064 + 5^2 \times 0.00032 - 1^2$$

$$= 0.8$$

On average, I would expect to be late one day a week with an expected variance of 0.8.

This worked example is a special case of the *binomial distribution*. This is used when a sequence of identical experiments, called trials, satisfy the following conditions:

1 Each trial has two outcomes (called success and failure).
2 The probabilities of success, p, and failure, $q = 1 - p$, are constant.
3 The outcomes of successive trials are independent.

If the total number of successes in n trials is denoted by X, we say that the random variable X follows the binomial distribution and write $X \sim B(n, p)$. The probability of getting r successes in n trials is given by

$$P(X = r) = {}^{n}C_r \times p^r \times q^{n-r}$$

because if there are r successes there must have been $n - r$ failures, and the number of ways in which this can occur is ${}^{n}C_r$.

The mean and variance of the $B(n, p)$ distribution are np and npq, respectively.

It is easy to see that the previous example is a special case of the above. The number of days in a week that I am late for work follows the $B(5, 0.2)$ distribution in which $n = 5$ and $p = 0.2$. As a check, notice that the general formulae for the mean and variance agree with the previous results:
$\mu = np = 5 \times 0.2 = 1$ and $\sigma^2 = npq = 5 \times 0.2 \times 0.8 = 0.8$.

Test yourself

Q5. Customers accessing a particular website are invited to complete an online survey. The probability that a person does this is 0.1. During the course of an hour, 20 people use the website. If the random variable X is the number of people who complete the survey during this time, state the distribution of X and calculate the mean and variance. What is the probability that during this hour:

(a) no-one completes the survey?

(b) exactly one person completes the survey?

(c) more than two people complete the survey?

Continuous random variables

Not all random variables take discrete values. Most physical quantities, such as height and time, can take all values in an interval, not just selected values such as whole numbers. In Figures 8.1 and 8.2, the distributions were illustrated using bars. For a continuous distribution, this is replaced by a curve. The area under the graph shown in Figure 8.3 gives the probability that the random variable takes values between a and b; because probabilities always add up to 1, the area under the complete graph must equal 1. There are two particular distributions that we are interested in – the *uniform* and *normal* distributions – and we consider each of these in turn.

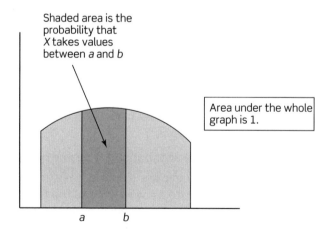

Figure 8.3

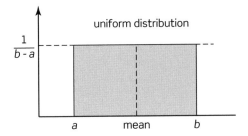

uniform distribution

$\dfrac{1}{b-a}$

a   mean   b

Figure 8.4

Uniform distribution

Figure 8.1 showed the probability distribution when a single die is rolled. The six outcomes are equally likely, so each bar has the same height. The corresponding diagram for a continuous random variable is shown in Figure 8.4. The probability is constant throughout the interval $a \le x \le b$. The width of the interval is $b - a$, so the height of the graph has to be

$$\dfrac{1}{b - a}$$

to ensure that the area under the rectangle is 1. The mean and variance of the distribution are given by

$$\mu = \dfrac{1}{2}(a + b)$$

and

$$\sigma^2 = \dfrac{1}{12}(a - b)^2.$$

The formula for the mean should come as no surprise to you because we know that whenever a data set or distribution is symmetrical, the mean and median coincide and are in the centre.

Worked example

The scheduled journey time on a train from King's Cross to Durham is 2 hours 54 minutes. In practice, the journey times vary between 2 hours 49 minutes and 3 hours 1 minute. Assuming that this can be modelled by a uniform distribution:

(a) find the mean and variance;

(b) calculate the probability that the train will arrive no later than 3 minutes after the scheduled time.

Solution

The distribution of times is shown in Figure 8.5. The width of the interval is 12 minutes so the height of the complete rectangle is 1/12.

(a) The mean is the mid-point, which is 2 hours 55 minutes. The variance is worked out from

$$\sigma^2 = \frac{1}{12}(a - b)^2 = \frac{1}{12} \times 12^2 = 12.$$

(b) If the train is 3 minutes late, the journey time is 2 hours 57 minutes. The probability that the time is less than this is the area of the shaded region in Figure 8.5. The region is a rectangle of width 8 and height 1/12, so the probability is 2/3.

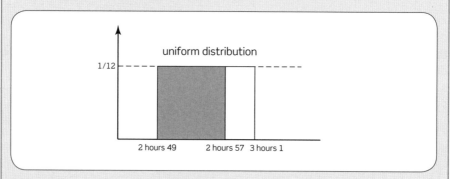

Figure 8.5

Test yourself

Q6. A machine weighs objects correct to the nearest 10 grams. It gives the weight of a packet of sweets as 70 grams. State the range of values of the true weight of the packet. Modelling the true weight by the uniform distribution:

(a) state the mean weight and calculate the standard deviation;

(b) find the probability that the packet weighs between 67 and 71 grams.

Normal distribution

The most useful probability distribution is the normal distribution. A selection of these distributions is sketched in Figure 8.6. Each curve is symmetrical and bell-shaped, centred on its mean, μ. The standard deviation, σ^2, governs the spread so influences the "steepness" of the bell. As σ^2 increases the bell widens out but, because the area under the curve is always 1, the height of the bell goes down. We write $X \sim N(\mu, \sigma^2)$ to indicate that a continuous random variable, X, follows a normal distribution with mean μ and variance σ^2. Figure 8.7 shows the probabilities of a normal variable taking values in intervals that are symmetrical about the mean. For example, Figure 8.7(b) shows that 95% of the population lies within 2 standard deviations either side of the mean. The curve is symmetric so the remaining 5% must be split equally, with each "tail" containing 2.5% of the whole population.

The normal distribution is important for three reasons. Firstly most numerical measures of natural phenomena are normally distributed. People's heights, weights and IQ all follow the normal distribution. Secondly, even if a population is not normally distributed then the means of large samples taken from it are normally distributed. We shall investigate this in the next two chapters. Finally it can be shown that provided the number of trials, n, is sufficiently large the binomial distribution, $B(n, p)$, can be approximated by the normal distribution, $N(np, npq)$. In practice this means that the probabilities obtained from the normal distribution provide a good approximation to the binomial probabilities provided that $np > 5$ and $nq > 5$.

The evaluation of areas under normal curves is mathematically very difficult. However, the use of normal tables (or a calculator) allows us to work out these probabilities easily. Rather than tabulate the probabilities for every possible

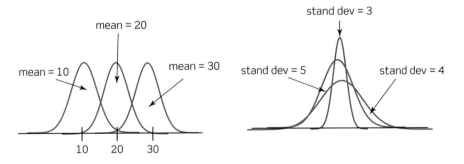

Figure 8.6

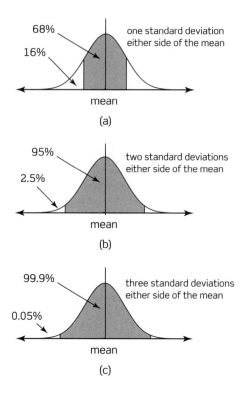

Figure 8.7

normal curve $N(\mu, \sigma^2)$ with each value of μ and σ^2, we perform a simple transformation that converts the problem into finding areas under the particular distribution, $N(0, 1)$. If $X \sim N(\mu, \sigma^2)$, the standardised variable,

$$Z = \frac{X - \mu}{\sigma},$$

which measures the number of standard deviations from the mean, follows the normal distribution with a mean, 0, and standard deviation, 1. An extract of the normal tables is given in Table 8.1 and the following worked example shows how to use it.

Table 8.1

z	0	1	2	3	4	5	6	7	8	9	1	2	3	4	5	6	7	8	9
0.5	.6915	.6950	.6985	.7019	.7054	.7088	.7123	.7157	.7190	.7224	3	7	10	14	17	20	24	27	31
0.6	.7257	.7291	.7324	.7357	.7389	.7422	.7454	.7486	.7517	.7549	3	7	10	13	16	19	23	26	29
0.7	.7580	.7611	.7642	.7673	.7704	.7734	.7764	.7794	.7823	.7852	3	6	9	12	15	18	21	24	27
0.8	.7881	.7910	.7939	.7967	.7995	.8023	.8051	.8078	.8106	.8133	3	5	8	11	14	16	19	22	25
0.9	.8159	.8186	.8212	.8238	.8264	.8289	.8315	.8340	.8365	.8389	5	5	8	10	13	15	18	20	23
1.0	.8413	.8438	.8461	.8485	.8508	.8531	.8554	.8577	.8599	.8621	2	4	6	8	10	12	14	16	18
1.1	.8643	.8665	.8686	.8708	.8729	.8749	.8770	.8790	.8810	.8830	2	4	6	7	9	11	13	15	17
1.2	.8849	.8869	.8888	.8907	.8925	.8944	.8962	.8980	.8997	.9015	2	3	5	6	8	10	11	13	14
1.3	.9032	.9049	.9066	.9082	.9099	.9115	.9131	.9147	.9162	.9177	1	3	4	6	7	8	10	11	13
1.4	.9192	.9207	.9222	.9236	.9251	.9265	.9279	.9292	.9306	.9319	1	2	4	5	6	7	8	10	11
1.5	.9332	.9345	.9357	.9370	.9382	.9394	.9406	.9418	.9429	.9441	1	2	3	4	5	6	7	8	9
1.6	.9452	.9463	.9474	.9484	.9495	.9505	.9515	.9525	.9535	.9545	1	2	3	4	5	6	7	8	9

Worked example

The hourly pay of a company's employees is known to be normally distributed with a mean of £24 and standard deviation of £3.

(a) Find the probability that an employee chosen at random from the company earns an hourly rate:
   (i)   of less than £27.75;
   (ii) of more than £26;
   (iii) between £26 and £27.75;
   (iv) of less than £22.

(b) The probability that a randomly chosen employee earns more than £x an hour is 0.05. Find the value of x.

Solution

If X is the random variable of the hourly pay then $X \sim N(24, 9)$ because the mean is 24 and variance is $3^2 = 9$. The standardised variable is

$$Z = \frac{X - 24}{3} \sim N(0, 1).$$

Table 8.1 shows the probability that the standardised variable Z takes values to the left of z under the N(0, 1) curve.

(a) (i)

$$P(X < 27.75) = P\left(\frac{X - 24}{3} < \frac{27.75 - 24}{3}\right) = P(Z < 1.25),$$

which is the area to the left of $z = 1.25$ in Figure 8.8. This can be found from the tables by locating the number in row 1.2 and column 5. This is highlighted in the extract in Table 8.1 and seen to be 0.8944.

(ii)

$$P(X > 26) = P\left(\frac{X - 24}{3} > \frac{26 - 24}{3}\right) = P(Z > 0.667)$$

is the area to the right of $z = 0.667$ in Figure 8.9. The total area under the graph is 1 so we can find the area to the left of 0.667 and then subtract from 1. This can be found by looking up the entry in row 0.6 and column 6, which is 0.7454, and then adding on 0.0023, which can be found in the last section of this row under column 7. This gives 0.7477 so the final answer is 0.2523.

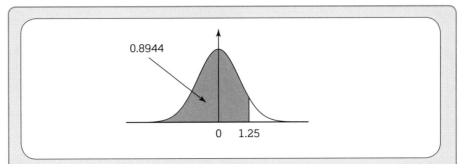

Figure 8.8

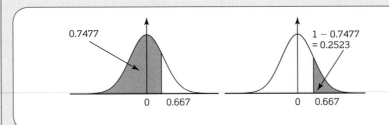

Figure 8.9

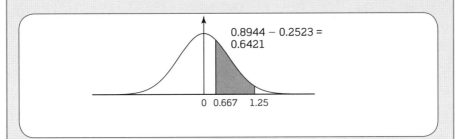

Figure 8.10

(iii) This is just the difference between the answers to parts (i) and (ii), as shown in Figure 8.10. $P(26 < X < 27.75) = P(0.667 < Z < 1.25) = 0.8944 - 0.2523 = 0.6421$.

(iv)

$$P(X < 22) = P\left(\frac{X - 24}{3} < \frac{22 - 24}{3}\right) = P(Z < -0.667).$$

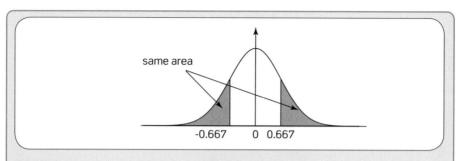

Figure 8.11

By symmetry of the graph of the normal distribution (illustrated in Figure 8.11), the area to the left of −0.667 is the same as the area to the right of 0.667, so the answer to this part of the question is the same as that to part (ii): 0.2523.

(b) In this part of the question we need to work backwards, finding the probability in the body of the table and then reading off the values from the header row and column. If the area to the right of x in Figure 8.12 is 0.05, then the area to the left is 0.95. From the tables we see that this occurs when the number of standard deviations above the mean is 1.645 so

$$\frac{x - 24}{3} = 1.645,$$

which gives $x = $ £28.94.

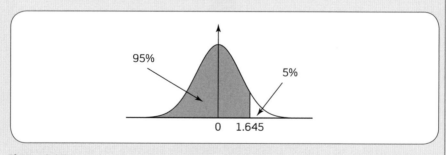

Figure 8.12

The value of the standardised variable that isolates the top or bottom 5% of the normal distribution is sometimes referred to as a *critical value* or *percentage point* of the distribution. Critical values are used widely in statistics and are often listed in a separate statistical table.

Test yourself

Q7. The time taken to drive to work is distributed normally, with mean 43 minutes and standard deviation 6 minutes.

(a) Find the probability of a journey time:

    (i) less than 45 minutes;

    (ii) more than 33 minutes;

    (iii) between 33 and 45 minutes.

(b) The probability of a journey time of less than x minutes is 0.0228. Find the value of x.

Chapter summary – pulling it all together

By the end of this chapter you should be able to:

	Confident ✓	Not confident?
Work out the number of choices using ^nC_r		Revise pages 141–142
Solve problems involving exclusive and independent events		Revise pages 142–143
Solve problems involving conditional probabilities using tree diagrams		Revise pages 143–145
Calculate the mean and variance of discrete distributions		Revise pages 145–149
Calculate probability, mean and variance of the binomial distribution, and know the conditions under which the model is valid		Revise pages 147–150
Work out probabilities, mean and variance of the uniform distribution		Revise pages 151–152
Use tables to evaluate probabilities associated with the normal distribution		Revise pages 153–159

Now try the assessment question at the start of the chapter using the answer guidelines below.

Answer guidelines

✳ Assessment question

Marks awarded on a course are known to be normally distributed with mean, μ, and standard deviation, σ. Based on these raw marks, degrees are classified as follows:

Marks	Degree classification
$x < 35$	Fail
$35 \leq x < 45$	Third
$45 \leq x < 56$	Lower second
$56 \leq x < 73$	Upper second
$x \geq 73$	First

(a) If 8% of candidates are awarded first class degrees, show that $1.406\sigma + \mu = 73$.

If 5% fail the course, write down a second equation and hence determine the values of μ and σ, correct to two decimal places.

(b) Show that 40.4% of candidates are awarded upper-second class degrees.

(c) Use the binomial distribution to calculate the probability that in a group of 10 students, exactly half have upper-second class degrees.

(d) Comment on the validity of using the binomial model in part (c).

Approaching the question

● This question is in four parts. You need the answer to the first part in order to answer the second part.

● It helps to draw a diagram in part (a). You produce two equations in two unknowns that need to be solved.

- Part (b) uses the values of μ and σ found in part (a). This provides a useful check that your answer to part (a) is correct.

- Part (c) uses the result of part (b), which was stated, so if you couldn't answer the earlier parts of the question you could still continue with the last two parts.

- The conditions of validity for the binomial distribution are listed on page 149. Work through each one in the context of this question. You are not being asked for a right or wrong answer here. This is your opportunity to convince the examiner that you are aware of the possible limitations of the model.

Method of solution

- Begin by defining your random variable X, and state its distribution. Write down the standardised variable, Z, in terms of X, μ and σ. Draw the normal curve and shade the regions representing the top 8% and bottom 5% of the area.

  - For the first equation, note that if 8% of the students are awarded first-class degrees, then 92% are not. Look up the number 0.92 in the body of the normal tables. The boundary between and first-class and upper-second class degree is stated in the question, so you can now use the formula for Z to derive the given equation.

  - For the second equation you can repeat the procedure using the fact that 5% of the area is below the fail boundary of 35.

  - Finally, you can solve the equations simultaneously to find μ and σ.

- Part (b) is quite easy. You need to find the probability of getting a mark between 56 and 73. You can do this by finding the difference between the areas under the normal curve to the left of 73 and 56. In fact, the area to the left of 73 can just be written down without further effort.

- For part (c), define your random variable and state, in the form $B(n,p)$, the specific binomial distribution that this random variable follows. The formula for calculating the probabilities for a binomial model is given on page 149.

- The binomial model can only be used when all three conditions listed on page 149 are satisfied. Tick them off mentally, and try to think of a reason why one or more of these might not be true in this case.

Companion website

Go to the companion website at **www.pearsoned.co.uk/econexpress** to find more revision support online for this topic area.

Notes

9 Sampling and estimation

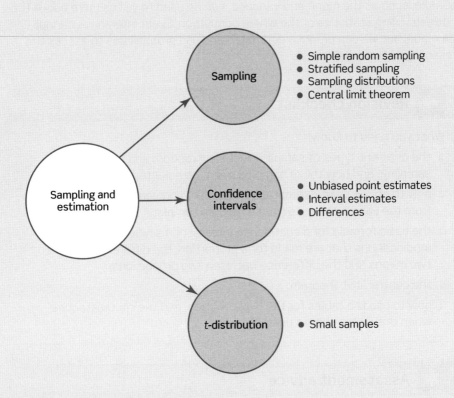

- Sampling
  - Simple random sampling
  - Stratified sampling
  - Sampling distributions
  - Central limit theorem

- Confidence intervals
  - Unbiased point estimates
  - Interval estimates
  - Differences

- t-distribution
  - Small samples

A printable version of this topic map is available from **www.pearsoned.co.uk/econexpress**

Introduction

In Chapter 7 we showed how a data set can be processed and analysed using measures of central tendency and measures of dispersion, and by illustrating data sets using suitable diagrams such as pie charts and histograms.

In practice, when investigating any sort of trends, it is unlikely that we would have access to a complete data set, known as the *parent population* (or simply the *population*); instead, we would select a subset of the data, known as the *sample*. For example, if we wanted to investigate national trends in household incomes, it would be far too costly and time-consuming to attempt to find out the income of every household in the country, so we would select a sample of households that would give us a representative picture of the population as a whole.

Inferential statistics is concerned with how information gleaned from a sample, such as the mean and variance, can be used to tell us more about the corresponding statistics of the whole population. Exact inferences cannot be made, but we can produce estimates and use probabilities to assess the reliability of these estimates.

 Revision checklist

What you need to know:
- the different types of sampling including random and stratified sampling, and how these samples might be selected in practice;
- how to obtain point estimates of the mean and variance of a population from the values obtained from a random sample;
- the basic formula for a confidence interval of a single mean, and the modifications that are made for a proportion, the difference between two means and the difference between two proportions;
- the central limit theorem;
- how to use the tables for the t-distribution, and the circumstances when this distribution is used.

✳ Assessment advice

- The sample variance provides a biased estimate of the population variance. To obtain an unbiased estimate you can work out the sample variance in the usual way, and then adjust it by multiplying by $n/(n - 1)$.
- Make sure that you interpret a confidence interval *correctly*.

- When tackling an exam question on confidence intervals, read the small print carefully before you begin. Are you told that the parent population is normal? If not, is the sample size large enough to justify using the central limit theorem? Do you know the population variance or do you need to estimate it from the sample variance?

- Remember to use the t-distribution for small samples when the exact value of the variance of the parent population is unknown. The parent population must be normally distributed and the sample random.

- Remember that, when finding the distribution for the differences between two sample means (or proportions), you *add* the standard deviations not subtract them.

✳ Assessment question

Could you answer this question? Guidelines on answering the question are presented at the end of this chapter.:

A chain of high-street cafes monitors its weekly sales of a particular type of coffee. Sales from a sample of 12 of its outlets are as follows:

93, 70, 122, 153, 98, 139, 141, 90, 92, 86, 99, 104

(a) Obtain unbiased estimates of the mean and standard deviation of weekly sales.

(b) Calculate the 95% confidence interval for the mean weekly sales. State clearly any assumptions that need to be made.

(c) Interpret your answer to part (b) carefully.

Management decides that it is only worthwhile to continue selling this particular coffee if the mean weekly sales exceed 100.

(d) What advice would you give, based on the answer to part (b)? Give brief reasons for your answer.

(e) In order to reduce the margin of error the company decides to repeat the survey using a larger sample. Estimate the smallest sample size needed to reduce the width of the 95% confidence interval to 10.

Sampling

Key definition

A sampling method in which every possible sample of fixed size has an equal chance of being selected is said to be **random**.

All of the results and tests that are used in statistical theory are based on the assumption that the selection process is random, so it is important that the sample has been chosen in this way.

To illustrate how such a sample could be found, suppose we wanted to canvas the views of students on a course. Each of the 600 students on the course (taken, for example, from an alphabetical list on a university database) could be allocated a number between 000 and 599. A computer-generated random number table is then used to define the sample. For example, suppose we wanted to pick a random sample of 30 students using the following random number table:

12 99 34 28 24 59 01 73 24 32 21 54 87 59 02 16 77 ...

Picking three digits from left to right, we obtain:

129 934 282 459 017 324 322 154 875 902 167 ...

Numbers that are not in the range 000 to 599 are ignored, thus giving a sample of students with numbers 129, 282, 459, and so on.

An alternative would be to use a system such as that adopted by the national lottery: balls numbered 000 to 599 are put into a machine, which then selects thirty of them at random.

Simple random sampling does produce a genuine random sample but it is important to realise that the sample will not always be a true representation of the population. For example, all 30 students might end up being chosen from the same year group, or they might all be mature students. Given that every possible sample has an equal chance of being selected, it must happen that an "extreme" sample is picked from time to time, in the same way that the numbers 1, 2, 3, 4, 5 and 6 could be picked in the national lottery.

To safeguard against this, a system of *stratified sampling* is sometimes used. The whole population is conveniently split into groups or "strata" that are quite different from each other (e.g. age groups, occupational groups, regional groups). Separate random samples are then selected from each stratum. Each group is represented proportionately in the sample. In the previous example, if a third of all students are from overseas then it might be appropriate to reflect this by picking 10 (out of the 30) students in the sample at random from this category. Stratified sampling gives more accurate results than simple random sampling when clear, non-overlapping strata are already present in the population. It also has the advantage of giving separate estimates for each group, which can be useful. The disadvantages are that the sample is not truly random and, in practice, the strata may overlap.

If we take random samples of fixed size n from a population, we would expect there to be some variation between the samples. To be specific, suppose the population consists of the weights of all 18-year-olds in the country, with a mean of 72 kg. From this population we pick a random sample of 100 and calculate the mean, x̄, of this sample. Each time we choose a different sample we get a different value of x̄. Although we would expect these sample means to be close to 72 kg, it is not impossible for a random sample to have a mean of, say, 100 kg when the sample is an extreme one. If we use X to denote the random variable "the weights of 18-year-olds" for the parent population, the sample means take different values with differing probabilities. Therefore the complete population of sample means, taken over all possible samples of the same size, can be represented by a random variable, $\overline{X}$. We have the following important result:

> If the distribution of a population, $X \sim N(\mu, \sigma^2)$ then the sample means, $\overline{X} \sim N(\mu, \sigma^2/n)$.

This shows that if the population is normal then the sample means are also normally distributed with the same mean, μ, but with variance σ^2/n. The standard deviation, $\sigma/\sqrt{n}$, is known as the *standard error*, and it confirms our intuition that the spread of sample means reduces as the size of the samples increase.

One obvious question to ask is: what happens when the distribution of a population is not normal (and perhaps not even known)? The good news is that, provided the sample size is large (30 or more), the sample means are normally distributed, regardless of the distribution of the population. This result is known as the *central limit theorem*.

Worked example

The weight of 18-year-olds is known to be normally distributed with mean 72 kg and standard deviation 8 kg. A random sample of 16 of these weights is chosen.

(a) What is the probability that the mean weight of this sample is below 67 kg?

(b) Is it necessary to use the central limit theorem to work out this probability?

Solution

(a) If X denotes the random variable consisting of the weights of 18-year-olds, then $X \sim N(72, 8^2)$. In this case, $n = 16$ so

$$\overline{X} \sim N\left(72, \frac{64}{16}\right) = N(72, 4).$$

If Z denotes the standardised variable, the probability that the sample mean is less than 67 can be worked out as follows:

$$P(\bar{X} < 67) = P\left(Z < \frac{67 - 72}{\sqrt{4}}\right)$$

$$= P(Z < -2.5)$$

$$= 1 - 0.9938$$

$$= 0.0062.$$

(b) We are told that the population from which the sample is drawn is normally distributed, so it is not necessary to use the central limit theorem. (In fact, the sample is too small to have used the central limit theorem anyway.)

Sometimes we are interested in estimating the proportion of a population that possesses a particular attribute. In politics, we might want to predict what proportion of adults in this country will vote Labour at the next general election; in employment, we need to know what proportion of people in work are part-time; in finance, auditors want to know what proportion of invoices are completed incorrectly. We can work out the proportion in a random sample that has the required attribute, and then consider how this sample proportion is distributed over all possible samples of fixed size, n. Provided n is sufficiently large, the sample proportion, P, is distributed normally. (In fact it is binomially distributed, but this can be approximated by the normal distribution provided np and nq both exceed 5, as mentioned in Chapter 8.) More precisely,

$$P \sim N\left(\pi, \frac{\pi(1 - \pi)}{n}\right)$$

where π is the true population proportion. Therefore, it is possible to work out the probabilities about sample proportions using the same method that we use for sample means.

Test yourself

Q1. The proportion of employees in a large company earning more than £30,000 a year is 46%. What is the probability that in a random sample of 30 of these employees, over half earn in excess of £30,000?

Confidence intervals

In the previous section, we considered the weights of 18-year-olds and used the true population mean to predict results for the sample mean. In practice, we work the other way round. We want to infer results about the population from the statistics of a sample. A random sample of size n is selected; the mean, $\bar{X}$, variance, s^2, and a proportion, p, of this sample are then found. Given that this is the only information available, would it be correct to use these three numbers as the best estimates of the mean, μ, variance, σ^2, and proportion, π, for the population? The three results below show that the answer is yes for the mean and proportion, but no for the variance.

1 $E(\bar{X}) = \mu$

2 $E(s^2) = \dfrac{n-1}{n} \times \sigma^2$

3 $E(P) = \pi$

Recall from Chapter 8 that the notation E is the expected value of a random variable. Result (1) shows that the expected value of the sample mean, taken over all possible samples, is the same as the population mean. In other words, although any individual sample mean may not be the true population mean, on average it is correct. We describe this by saying that the sample mean is unbiased as it provides an unbiased estimate of the population mean. Result (3) shows the sample proportion is also unbiased because, on average, the sample proportion is the population proportion. However, result (2) indicates that the sample variance is biased, because the expected value of the sample variance is not σ^2. In fact, result 2 can be rearranged as

$$\frac{n}{n-1}E(s^2) = \sigma^2,$$

which shows that an unbiased estimate of the population variance can be obtained by multiplying the sample variance by $n/(n-1)$. Recall from Chapter 7 that the sample variance is defined as

$$s^2 = \frac{1}{n}\sum_{i=1}^{n}(x_i - \bar{x})^2,$$

so an unbiased estimate of σ^2 is

$$\frac{n}{n-1} \times \frac{1}{n}\sum_{i=1}^{n}(x_i - \bar{x})^2 = \frac{1}{n-1}\sum_{i=1}^{n}(x_i - \bar{x})^2.$$

This looks like the same formula but with $n-1$ in place of n. For this reason the sample variance is often labelled σ_n on a calculator to distinguish it from the estimate of the population variance, which is labelled as σ_{n-1}.

Worked example

A random sample of 20 people is chosen from the population of 18-year-olds in this country. The weights (in kg) of these people are:

65, 59, 68, 65, 67, 71, 72, 71, 67, 65, 74, 66, 92, 68, 63, 66, 70, 69, 83, 69

(a) Find unbiased estimates for the population mean and variance.

(b) Estimate the proportion of 18-year-olds in this country who weigh more than 80 kg.

Solution

(a) We begin by finding the sample mean and sample variance:

$$\bar{x} = \frac{\sum x}{n} = \frac{1390}{20} = 69.5$$

and

$$s^2 = \frac{1}{n}\sum x^2 - (\bar{x})^2 = \frac{97580}{20} - 69.5^2 = 48.75$$

so unbiased estimates of the mean and variance are $\mu = 69.5$ and

$$\sigma^2 = \frac{20}{19} \times 48.75 = 51.32.$$

(b) The number of students in the sample weighing more than 80 kg is 2, so an unbiased estimate of the proportion for the whole population of 18-year-olds is $\pi = \frac{2}{20} = 10\%$.

Test yourself

Q2. A random sample of 15 people in a large company are asked how many hours overtime they work each week. The results are summarised as $\sum x = 81$ and $\sum x^2 = 587$. Find unbiased estimates of the mean and variance of number of hours' overtime for the whole company from which this sample is drawn.

The previous worked example produced (point) estimates for the population mean and proportion. It is often more useful to give a range of values within which μ or π lie with a particular degree of certainty. We know from the previous section that if the parent population is normal (or when the sample size $n \geq 30$ so that the central limit theorem can be used) the sample means are normally distributed with mean μ and variance σ^2/n. From the normal tables, we know that 95% of the values in a normal distribution lie within 1.96 standard deviations of the mean. Hence there is a 95% chance that the sample mean, $\bar{x}$, will be in the range

$$\mu - 1.96\frac{\sigma}{\sqrt{n}} < \bar{x} < \mu + 1.96\frac{\sigma}{\sqrt{n}}.$$

This can be rearranged to give

$$\bar{x} - 1.96\frac{\sigma}{\sqrt{n}} < \mu < \bar{x} + 1.96\frac{\sigma}{\sqrt{n}}.$$

Key definition

The 95% **confidence interval** for a population mean is the range from

$$\bar{x} - 1.96\frac{\sigma}{\sqrt{n}} \text{ to } \bar{x} + 1.96\frac{\sigma}{\sqrt{n}}.$$

Notice that a confidence interval varies with each sample mean. If you were to write down all possible confidence intervals (one for each possible sample) then the true population mean would lie in 95% of them. It follows that there is a 5% chance that any one particular confidence interval does not contain the mean.

Other confidence intervals are possible. The normal tables show that 90% and 99% of a normal variable lies within 1.645 and 2.576 standard deviations of the mean, respectively.

The 90% confidence interval for a population mean is the range from

$$\bar{x} - 1.645\frac{\sigma}{\sqrt{n}} \text{ to } \bar{x} + 1.645\frac{\sigma}{\sqrt{n}}$$

and the 99% confidence interval for a population mean is the range from

$$\bar{x} - 2.576\frac{\sigma}{\sqrt{n}} \text{ to } \bar{x} + 2.576\frac{\sigma}{\sqrt{n}}.$$

Notice that, as expected, a 99% confidence interval is wider than a 95% confidence interval: if a greater percentage of intervals are going to include the population mean then the interval has to be more generous.

We noted in the previous section that, provided n is sufficiently large, the population proportion is also normally distributed:

$$P \sim N\left(\pi, \frac{\pi(1 - \pi)}{n}\right)$$

The 95% confidence interval for the population proportion is the range from

$$p - 1.96\sqrt{\frac{\pi(1 - \pi)}{n}} \text{ to } p + 1.96\sqrt{\frac{\pi(1 - \pi)}{n}}.$$

Notice that the calculation of the interval involves π, which is precisely the statistic that we are trying to estimate! We can avoid this difficulty by estimating the confidence intervals using the sample proportion p (which is an unbiased estimate) in place of π.

Worked example

In a random sample of 60 employees of a large company, 15 are part-time.

(a) Estimate a 95% confidence interval for the proportion of part-time employees in the firm.

(b) What size sample should be taken to reduce the width of this confidence interval to 0.1?

Solution

(a) In this case, $n = 60$ and

$$p = \frac{15}{60} = 0.25.$$

As mentioned earlier we do not know the exact population proportion, π, so we estimate it using the sample proportion, $p = 0.25$. The confidence interval (rounded to two significant figures) is from

$$0.25 - 1.96\sqrt{\frac{0.25(1 - 0.25)}{60}} = 0.14$$

to

$$0.25 + 1.96\sqrt{\frac{0.25(1 - 0.25)}{60}} = 0.36.$$

The numbers 0.14 and 0.36 are called the *confidence limits* and the confidence interval itself can be written as (0.14, 0.36).

(b) In general the width of a 95% confidence interval for a proportion is

$$2 \times 1.96\sqrt{\frac{\pi(1 - \pi)}{n}}.$$

In this case, $\pi \approx 0.25$ so we want to choose the sample size, n, so that

$$3.92\sqrt{\frac{0.1875}{n}} = 0.1.$$

This equation can be solved to get

$$n = \left(\frac{3.92}{0.1}\right)^2 \times 0.1875 = 288.12$$

so we would need to sample 289 employees to reduce the width of the interval to 0.1.

Test yourself

Q3. Twenty households keep a record of how much they spend on groceries in a month and the mean is calculated to be £380. The standard deviation of the population is known to be £16. Calculate the 90% confidence interval for the mean and state clearly any assumptions that need to be made.

As well as finding the confidence intervals of individual means (and proportions), it is sometimes useful to construct confidence intervals for the *differences* between two means (and proportions). In a company, we are interested in the difference in the mean hourly rate of pay of full- and part-time employees; in politics, we might wish to find the difference between the proportions of men and women who vote for a particular party. It can be shown that provided two normal variables are independent, their difference is also normally distributed.

More precisely, if

$$\overline{X}_1 \sim N\left(\mu_1, \frac{\sigma_1^2}{n_1}\right)$$

and

$$\overline{X}_2 \sim N\left(\mu_2, \frac{\sigma_2^2}{n_2}\right)$$

then

$$\overline{X}_1 - \overline{X}_2 \sim N\left(\mu_1 - \mu_2, \frac{\sigma_1^2}{n_1} + \frac{\sigma_2^2}{n_2}\right)$$

The 95% confidence interval for the difference between two means ranges from

$$(\bar{x}_1 - \bar{x}_2) - 1.96\sqrt{\frac{\sigma_1^2}{n_1} + \frac{\sigma_2^2}{n_2}}$$

to

$$(\bar{x}_1 - \bar{x}_2) + 1.96\sqrt{\frac{\sigma_1^2}{n_1} + \frac{\sigma_2^2}{n_2}}.$$

Notice that the interval is centred on the *difference* between the sample means, but the margin of error involves the *sum* of the standard deviations. In order for this result to be valid it is necessary for the two samples to be independent; if you wanted to find the difference between the salary of men and women you must *not* choose samples from married couples because these cannot be independent.

Proportions behave in the same way.

The 95% confidence interval for the difference between two proportions ranges from

$$(p_1 - p_2) - 1.96\sqrt{\frac{\pi_1(1 - \pi_1)}{n_1} + \frac{\pi_2(1 - \pi_2)}{n_2}}$$

to

$$(p_1 - p_2) + 1.96\sqrt{\frac{\pi_1(1 - \pi_1)}{n_1} + \frac{\pi_2(1 - \pi_2)}{n_2}}.$$

Worked example

A company sells clothes both in its high street stores and on the internet. The amount of money that a customer spends in single transactions is normally distributed, with standard deviations of £18 and £20 for in-store and online shopping, respectively. The mean spend of a random sample of 20 in-store shoppers is £64, compared to £51 for a random sample of 25 transactions online.

(a) Find a 95% confidence interval for the difference in the means.

(b) Does this provide evidence that people spend more on average when they visit a shop rather than buying online?

Solution

(a) In this case, $n_1 = 20$, $n_2 = 25$; $\bar{x}_1 = 64$, $\bar{x}_2 = 51$; $\sigma_1^2 = 18^2$, $\sigma_2^2 = 20^2$.

The point estimate for the difference between the means is $\bar{x}_1 - \bar{x}_2 = 64 - 51 = 13$ and the confidence interval ranges from

$$13 - 1.96\sqrt{\frac{18^2}{20} + \frac{20^2}{25}} = 1.88$$

to

$$13 + 1.96\sqrt{\frac{18^2}{20} + \frac{20^2}{25}} = 24.12.$$

(b) The values in the confidence interval (1.88, 24.12) are all positive, providing reasonable evidence that the mean spend in a shop is greater than the mean spend online. Of course, we cannot be certain of this: by definition, with a 95% confidence interval there is a probability of 0.05 that the true difference lies outside any one particular interval.

Test yourself

Q4. In a random sample of 40 men, 18 preferred to shop online instead of visiting a store in person. The corresponding figure for a random sample of 50 women was 14.

    (a) Find a 95% confidence interval for the difference between the proportions.

    (b) Does this provide evidence that a greater proportion of men prefer to shop online than women?

t-distribution

You may have noticed that the formula for confidence intervals of a mean involves the population variance, σ^2. In practice this statistic may not be known. An obvious way forward is to replace the true population variance σ^2 with the unbiased estimate S^2, obtained from the sample:

$$S^2 = \frac{n}{n-1} \times \text{sample variance.}$$

If we make this switch from σ^2 to S^2 then the standardised variable,

$$Z = \frac{\overline{X} - \mu}{S/\sqrt{n}},$$

no longer follows the $N(0, 1)$ distribution. Provided the parent population is normally distributed, it can be shown that Z follows the (Student's) t-distribution instead. This distribution is not that dissimilar to the normal distribution: the general shape of this distribution is also a symmetric bell-shaped curve centred on zero, and there are tables that we can use to work out probabilities. The main difference is that the distributions depend on the sample size. For the normal distribution we know that 95% of the population always lies within 1.96 standard deviations from the mean. However, for the t-distribution, confidence intervals for a mean range from $\overline{x} - t \times S/\sqrt{n}$ to $\overline{x} + t \times S/\sqrt{n}$, where the number t depends on both the level of confidence and the size of the sample.

Figure 9.1 shows a typical t-distribution. The shaded area gives the probability, p, and the value of t indicates the number of standard deviations above the mean. Table 9.1 shows part of the t-tables. Each row of the table relates to v, the *number of degrees of freedom*. In the application considered here, $v = n - 1$; it is one fewer than the sample size.

As an example, suppose we wanted to find the 95% confidence interval based on a sample size of 15. A confidence interval is symmetric, so each tail in Figure 9.2 contains 2.5% of the distribution.

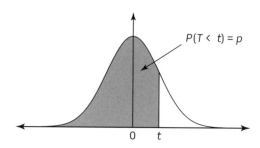

Figure 9.1

Table 9.1

p	0.75	0.90	0.95	0.975	0.99	0.995	0.9975	0.999	0.9995
13	0.694	1.350	1.771	2.160	2.650	3.012	3.372	3.852	4.221
14	0.692	1.345	1.761	2.145	2.624	2.997	3.326	3.787	4.140
15	0.691	1.341	1.753	2.131	2.602	2.947	3.286	3.733	4.073
16	0.690	1.337	1.746	2.120	2.583	2.921	3.252	3.686	4.015
...									
120	0.677	1.289	1.658	1.980	2.358	2.617	2.860	3.160	3.373
∞	0.674	1.282	1.645	1.960	2.326	2.576	2.807	3.090	3.291

Therefore, the total area shaded in Figure 9.1 needs to be 0.975. The number of degrees of freedom is $\nu = 15 - 1 = 14$. The corresponding value of t, shaded in Table 9.1, is 2.145 so the 95% confidence interval goes from $\bar{x} - 2.145 \times S/\sqrt{15}$ to $\bar{x} + 2.145 \times S/\sqrt{15}$.

This is wider than the 95% confidence interval for the normal distribution, reflecting the fact that the presence of S introduces an extra element of uncertainty. Notice from the numbers in the bottom rows of Table 9.1 that, for large samples, the values of t are the same as those used for the normal distribution considered previously, so it is only necessary to use the t-distribution when the sample sizes are small.

The t-distribution can also be used to estimate confidence intervals for the difference of the means of two distributions. The conditions under which the procedure is valid are as follows:

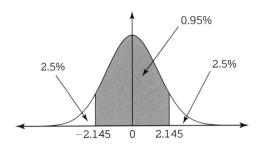

Figure 9.2

- The two samples must be random and independent of each other.
- Both populations are normally distributed.
- The population variances must be assumed to be the same for both distributions. An unbiased estimate of this common variance (known as the pooled variance) is calculated from the two samples together, using $S^2 = (n_1 s_1^2 + n_2 s_2^2)/(n_1 + n_2 - 2)$, where s_1 and s_2 are the original sample variances.

  If you use the unbiased estimates of the sample variances S_1^2 and S_2^2 instead, the formula becomes $S^2 = ((n_1 - 1)S_1^2 + (n_2 - 1)S_2^2)/(n_1 + n_2 - 2)$.

- The number of degrees of freedom is given by $v = n_1 + n_2 - 2$.

The confidence interval for the difference in the means ranges from

$$(\bar{x}_1 - \bar{x}_2) - t\sqrt{\frac{S^2}{n_1} + \frac{S^2}{n_2}} = (\bar{x}_1 - \bar{x}_2) - tS\sqrt{\frac{1}{n_1} + \frac{1}{n_2}}$$

to

$$(\bar{x}_1 - \bar{x}_2) + t\sqrt{\frac{S^2}{n_1} + \frac{S^2}{n_2}} = (\bar{x}_1 - \bar{x}_2) + tS\sqrt{\frac{1}{n_1} + \frac{1}{n_2}},$$

where the appropriate value of t is found from the t-tables.

Worked example

A random sample of seven men in a large firm earns an average of £25,560 a year, with standard deviation £2,450. The corresponding figures for 11 women are £23,950 and £1,970. Assuming that the salaries for men and women are normally distributed, estimate a 90% confidence interval for the difference in mean salaries between men and women in this firm. Does this provide evidence that men earn more than women in this firm?

Solution

The point estimate of the difference between the means is

    25560 – 23950 = £1610.

The number of degrees of freedom, $v = 7 + 11 - 2 = 16$.

The pooled variance,

$$S^2 = \frac{7 \times 2450^2 + 11 \times 1970^2}{16} = 5294212.5,$$

so $S = £2,301$.

For a 90% confidence interval, each tail is 5% so the area to the left of t is 0.95.

Table 9.1 shows that the value of t is 1.746 so the confidence interval ranges from

$$1610 - 1.746 \times 2301 \times \sqrt{\frac{1}{7} + \frac{1}{11}} = -332$$

to

$$1610 + 1.746 \times 2301 \times \sqrt{\frac{1}{7} + \frac{1}{11}} = 3552,$$

i.e. the 90% confidence interval for the difference in mean salaries is (−332, 3552).

This is a 90% interval so there is a 1 in 10 chance that the difference between the mean salaries lies outside the range. Also the interval itself includes negative numbers, so this provides no evidence that in this firm men earn higher average salaries.

Test yourself

Q5. Examination marks for the first-year quantitative methods paper are known to be normally distributed. The mean and standard deviation of a random sample of 14 scripts are 62 and 9, respectively. Estimate the 95% confidence interval for the mean mark of all students on this paper.

Chapter summary – pulling it all together

By the end of this chapter you should be able to:

	Confident ✓	Not confident?
Know how to obtain a simple random sample and a stratified sample		Revise page 166
Calculate the distributions of the sample means and population proportions		Revise pages 167–168
Use the central limit theorem		Revise pages 167–168

	Confident ✓	Not confident?
Calculate unbiased estimates of a population mean, variance and proportion		Revise pages 169–170
Understand what is meant by a confidence interval		Revise pages 170–171
Find confidence intervals for means and proportions		Revise pages 171–175
Know how and when to use the t-distribution		Revise pages 176–179

Now try the assessment question at the start of the chapter using the answer guidelines below.

Answer guidelines

✻ Assessment question

A large chain of high-street cafes monitors its weekly sales of a particular type of coffee. Sales from a sample of 12 of its outlets are as follows:

     93, 70, 122, 153, 98, 139, 141, 90, 92, 86, 99, 104

(a) Obtain unbiased estimates of the mean and standard deviation of weekly sales.

(b) Calculate the 95% confidence interval for the mean weekly sales. State clearly any assumptions that need to be made.

(c) Interpret your answer to part (b) carefully.

Management decides that it is only worthwhile to continue selling this particular coffee if the mean weekly sales exceed 100.

(d) What advice would you give, based on the answer to part (b)? Give brief reasons for your answer.

(e) In order to reduce the margin of error the company decides to repeat the survey using a larger sample. Estimate the smallest sample size needed to reduce the width of the 95% confidence interval to 10.

Approaching the question

- This question is in five parts that are interlinked.
- Decide at the beginning exactly what individual steps are needed to tackle each part.
- Read the whole question through carefully and note all relevant features that are mentioned. Is the sample small or large? Do you know the population variance or will you need to estimate it from the sample? Is this a question on the normal distribution or the t-distribution?
- Make a note of any conditions that are missing from the question that are necessary to justify the use of the statistical procedure.
- Although there are no watertight checks you can perform to guarantee that you have made no mistakes, you should at least make sure that your answers seem sensible before moving on to the next part.

Method of solution

- The sample mean automatically provides an unbiased estimate whereas, for the variance, you need to remember to either use the factor of $n/(n - 1)$ or use the σ_{n-1} button on your calculator (not σ_n).
- A worked example showing you how to find unbiased estimates is given on page 170.
- In this question the population variance is unknown and the sample is small, so you must use the t-distribution.
  - The general formula for a confidence interval is given on page 176.
  - Use of confidence intervals is only valid for certain types of samples. If these are not specified in the question then you must state them.
  - Use of the t-distribution is only valid under certain conditions. Again, you must state these if they have not been given.
- In part (c) the examiner is just checking that you know what a confidence interval really is. Try to put your answer in context.
- Remember that you can never make categorical statements when interpreting confidence intervals but you can make sensible judgements based on statistical evidence. You need to give a balanced answer to part (d) that convinces the examiner that you appreciate this.

- The last part is quite difficult to do if you use the t-distribution because the width of a confidence interval changes with sample size. You can avoid this dilemma by switching to the normal distribution, but you need to justify this change.

Companion website

Go to the companion website at **www.pearsoned.co.uk/econexpress** to find more revision support online for this topic area.

Notes

10 Hypothesis testing

Topic map

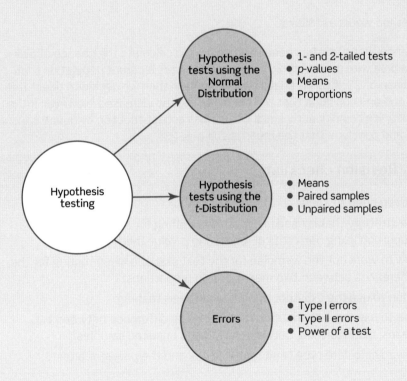

- Hypothesis tests using the Normal Distribution
  - 1- and 2-tailed tests
  - p-values
  - Means
  - Proportions

- Hypothesis tests using the t-Distribution
  - Means
  - Paired samples
  - Unpaired samples

- Errors
  - Type I errors
  - Type II errors
  - Power of a test

A printable version of this topic map is available from **www.pearsoned.co.uk/econexpress**

Introduction

In hypothesis testing a statement is made about a population, and we investigate whether this is supported by evidence collected from a sample. This statement usually involves the proposition that the mean or proportion of a population has changed recently.

As an example, we might know that in the past the average number of hours each week that a student spends on the internet is 23. However, lecturers believe that this number has increased, and they decide to put it to the test by finding the average time for a random sample of 40 students. Suppose that the mean of the sample turns out to be 26 hours. Does this provide evidence that the mean for the whole population has increased or could the increase be explained away as a "rogue" sample? The truth is, of course, that we cannot ever be certain, but we can make an informed decision based on probabilities.

The method works as follows.

We assume that there has been no change, and calculate the chance of picking a sample with a mean of 26 hours or more from a parent population that has a mean of 23. If this probability is very small, then we decide to reject the status quo and conclude that the mean has indeed increased. However, if the probability isn't significantly small we will just accept that the evidence is insufficient, and conclude that the mean is still only 23.

 Revision checklist

What you need to know:

- ❑ the strategy that is used in hypothesis testing for a single mean and proportion using both critical region and *p*-value methods;
- ❑ how to work out the formulae for the test statistic when testing for the differences between two means or two proportions;
- ❑ when to use the *t*-distribution for hypothesis testing;
- ❑ how to use the *t*-distribution for testing the difference between two means, distinguishing between paired and unpaired samples;
- ❑ how to calculate type I and type II errors, and the power of a test.

❊ Assessment advice

- Make sure that you state each of the following in your answers:
  - the random variable being investigated;
  - null and alternative hypotheses;

- distribution of the test statistic assuming that H_0 is true;
- rejection region;
- value of the test statistic;
- conclusion of the test, which should include the significance level and be set in context.
- Check that the conditions required to perform a test are either provided in the question or stated in your answer. For the t-test for
  - a single mean, the population must be normally distributed;
  - a paired test, the differences must be normally distributed;
  - an unpaired test, both populations are normally distributed, the variances of both populations are the same and the samples are independent.

✳ Assessment question

Could you answer this question? Guidelines on answering the question are presented at the end of this chapter.

Prices of return flights to New York are normally distributed with standard deviation £100. An airline's advertising brochure claims that the average price is as low as £678. To test this claim a random sample of 20 flights are chosen, which give a mean price of £720.

(a) Test the airline's claim at the 5% level.

(b) What would the minimum significance level need to be to reject the null hypothesis for this particular sample?

(c) What assumptions or modifications (if any) would need to be made to the test when:

  (i) the population is not normal, the standard deviation of the population is given and a random sample of 50 flights is used;

  (ii) the population is normal but the standard deviation of the population is unknown, and the sample size is 20.

(d) It is decided to investigate the following hypotheses: H_0: μ = £678 and H_1: μ = £720. Assuming that the flight prices are normally distributed with standard deviation £100, what sample size must be tested so that the probabilities of making a type I and type II error are 5% and 10%, respectively?

Hypothesis tests using the Normal Distribution

Key definitions

Null hypothesis: a statement, H_0, that a population statistic takes a particular value.

Alternative hypothesis: a statement, H_1, that the statistic being tested has increased, decreased or just changed, from the value given in the null hypothesis.

Test statistic: number that you calculate from the sample in order to test out the null hypothesis.

Critical (or rejection) region: the range of values of the test statistic, which leads to the rejection of the null hypothesis.

Significance level: the probability that the test statistic is in the critical region.

Worked example

The mean and standard deviation of the time taken to perform a task are 24 and 9 minutes, respectively. A management consultancy firm makes a series of recommendations designed to reduce the average time for an employee to complete the task.

After these recommendations are implemented, a random sample of 36 times are taken and the mean is found to be 21 minutes.

Test at the 5% level the claim that the mean times have decreased.

Solution

Let X be the random variable consisting of the times taken to complete the task.

In this example, the statement concerns the population mean. The original mean is known to be 24 minutes, and we are testing to see whether the new system has reduced this figure, so the null and alternative hypotheses are $H_0: \mu = 24$ and $H_1: \mu < 24$.

Although we are not told that the population times are normally distributed, the sample size is large ($n > 30$) so the central limit theorem shows that the sample means can be assumed to be normally distributed, i.e. that

$$\bar{X} \sim N\left(\mu, \frac{\sigma^2}{n}\right).$$

We now assume that the null hypothesis is true and investigate the consequence of this.

If $\mu = 24$, $n = 36$ and $\sigma^2 = 9^2 = 81$, then the sample means,

$$\bar{X} \sim N\left(24, \frac{81}{36}\right) = N(24, 2.25),$$

so

$$Z = \frac{\bar{X} - 24}{\sqrt{2.25}} \sim N(0, 1)$$

The significance level is 5% so we will reject the null hypothesis whenever the value of the standardised variable, z, lies in the shaded area shown in Figure 10.1. From the normal tables the critical value of z is −1.645 so we will reject H_0 if $z < -1.645$.

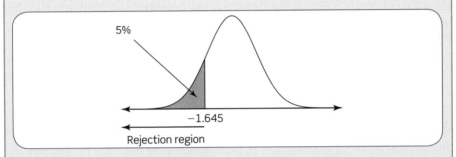

Figure 10.1

In this case, the sample mean, $\bar{x} = 21$, so the test statistic is

$$z = \frac{21 - 24}{1.5} = -2.$$

This lies inside the rejection region, so we reject H_0 and accept H_1.

We conclude that at the 5% significance level, there is sufficient evidence to suggest that the average time taken to complete the task has decreased.

Notice that we must specify the significance level in our conclusion because it provides a measure of certainty. In this case there is a 5% chance that the population mean really is still 24 minutes and the apparent reduction in the average time is caused by an unrepresentative sample.

The decision could be made stronger by using a smaller significance level such as 1%. This would give a rejection region of $z < -2.326$ so in this case the null hypothesis would actually be accepted.

Alternative approach

An alternative method of hypothesis testing is based on the so-called p-value (or probability value) of the test statistic. For the previous example, we use the normal tables to calculate the probability that the standardised normal variable, Z, takes values below the test statistic, −2 (or equivalently that the sample means are less than 21 minutes). In this case $P(Z < -2) = 1 - 0.9772 = 0.0218 = 2.18\%$.

As this is under 5% we must be in the critical region, so we reject H_0. In fact, we can deduce that the null hypothesis would be rejected for all significance levels over 2.18%.

In this worked example we were interested in finding out whether the mean times had been reduced, producing a rejection region in the left-hand tail of the normal curve shown in Figure 10.1. If we want to investigate a possible increase in the mean, then the rejection region lies in the right-hand tail, as shown in Figure 10.2. Sometimes we are only interested in a change in the mean without specifying whether it is an increase or a decrease. In this case the rejection region occupies both tails. If the significance level is 5% then each tail is 2.5%, as shown in Figure 10.3. We need to use the normal tables to find the value of Z corresponding to a probability of 0.975. The rejection region is $|z| > 1.96$.

Hypothesis tests based on Figure 10.1 or 10.2 are called *one-tailed* whereas those based on Figure 10.3 are called *two-tailed*.

The worked example showed how to perform a hypothesis test for a mean. The same procedure can be used for a proportion. Recall that provided n is large (that is, $n\pi > 5$ and $n(1 - \pi) > 5$) the sample proportions,

$$P \sim N\left(\pi, \frac{\pi(1 - \pi)}{n}\right),$$

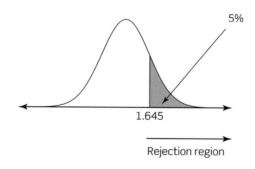

5%

1.645

Rejection region

Figure 10.2

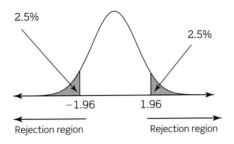

Figure 10.3

where π is the population proportion. The standardised test statistic is then

$$Z = \frac{P - \pi}{\sqrt{\dfrac{\pi(1 - \pi)}{n}}} \quad \text{where } Z \sim N(0, 1)$$

Test yourself

Q1. In the past few years, 25% of a company's orders have been exported to China. In a random sample of 80 orders, it is found that 16 are exported to China. Test, at the 5% level, whether the proportion has changed.

In Chapter 9 we showed how to find the confidence interval for the difference between two means and the difference between two proportions. The results used there extend in an obvious way to hypothesis testing.

Worked example

In a random sample of 150 men, 42 say that they will vote for the Labour Party at the next election. In a random sample of 225 women this number is 90.

Test at the 5% level whether there is difference between the voting intentions of men and women in this country.

Solution

Let π_1 and π_2 denote respectively the proportion of men and women who intend to vote for the Labour Party.

If P_1 and P_2 denote the corresponding proportions in random samples comprising n_1 men and n_2 women then, because both samples are large,

$$P_1 \sim N\left(\pi_1, \frac{\pi_1(1 - \pi_1)}{n_1}\right)$$

and

$$P_2 \sim N\left(\pi_2, \frac{\pi_2(1 - \pi_2)}{n_2}\right)$$

If the samples are independent then

$$P_1 - P_2 \sim N\left(\pi_1 - \pi_2, \frac{\pi_1(1 - \pi_1)}{n_1} + \frac{\pi_2(1 - \pi_2)}{n_2}\right)$$

The null and alternative hypotheses are $H_0: \pi_1 - \pi_2 = 0$ and $H_1: \pi_1 - \pi_2 \neq 0$.

If we assume that the null hypothesis is true, there is no difference between the proportions so we can write $\pi_1 = \pi_2 = \pi$, say, so that

$$P_1 - P_2 \sim N\left(0, \pi(1 - \pi)\left(\frac{1}{n_1} + \frac{1}{n_2}\right)\right)$$

The standardised test statistic is

$$Z = \frac{P_1 - P_2 - 0}{\sqrt{\pi(1 - \pi)\left(\frac{1}{n_1} + \frac{1}{n_2}\right)}} \sim N(0, 1).$$

For a two-tailed test at the 5% level, the critical region is $|z| > 1.96$.

In this case $n_1 = 150$, $n_2 = 225$;

$$P_1 = \frac{42}{150} = 0.28,$$

$$P_2 = \frac{90}{225} = 0.4.$$

In order to work out the value of the test statistic we need the value of π, which is unknown. The best we can do is to estimate it using all of the available data. Out of a total of 375 people, 132 say that they will vote Labour so we estimate π to be $132 \div 375 = 0.352$.

The value of the test statistic is

$$z = \frac{0.28 - 0.4 - 0}{\sqrt{0.352(1 - 0.352)\left(\frac{1}{150} + \frac{1}{225}\right)}} = -2.38.$$

This is inside the critical region so we conclude that at the 5% level there is significant evidence of a difference between the proportions of men and women intending to vote Labour.

Test yourself

Q2. Two colleges enter candidates for the same examination. The variance of the marks for College A is 40. For College B it is 30.

Random samples produce the following results table:

College	Sample size	Sample mean
A	100	38.3
B	80	40.1

Test, at the 5% level, whether the average marks for the two colleges are significantly different.

Hypothesis tests using the *t*-Distribution

As noted in Chapter 9, whenever the variance, σ^2, of the parent population is unknown we can replace it by an unbiased estimate, S^2, obtained from the sample. The sample means are no longer normally distributed. Instead, provided the parent population is normal, the test statistic

$$\frac{\overline{X} - \mu}{S/\sqrt{n}}$$

follows the *t*-distribution with $n - 1$ degrees of freedom. For large values of n, the distribution of t approximates closely to the normal distribution, so the *t*-distribution need only be used for small samples.

Worked example

A large company in the IT industry claims that the average salary of its employees is £34,000.

The mean and standard deviation of a random sample of 16 employees is £29,500 and £6,000, respectively. A prospective employee is concerned that the company's figure of £34,000 might be too high.

Test, at the 1% level, whether this concern is justified. State any assumptions required to carry out the test.

Solution

Let X be the random variable representing the annual salaries of employees in the firm. An unbiased estimate of the variance of X is

$$S^2 = \frac{16}{15} \times 6000^2 = 38,400,000$$

giving $S = 6197$.

The hypotheses are $H_0: \mu = 34,000$ and $H_1: \mu < 34,000$.

Under H_0 the test statistic,

$$T = \frac{\overline{X} - 34,000}{6197/\sqrt{16}}$$

follows the t-distribution with 15 degrees of freedom. The t-tables indicate that, for a one-tailed test at the 1% level, the critical region is $t < -2.602$.

The value of the test statistic is

$$t = \frac{29,500 - 34,000}{6197/\sqrt{16}} = -2.90,$$

which is in the critical region.

At the 1% level there is significant evidence that the mean salary of the company is less than the advertised value of £34,000.

We need to assume that the salaries of all employees in the firm are normally distributed for the t-test to be valid.

We can use the t-distribution to test for the difference between two means, although the procedure varies according to whether the samples are paired or unpaired. The distinction between these is most easily understood using examples.

Unpaired samples

Worked example

The table below shows the weekly number of telephone sales made by a random selection of employees who work for two different energy companies.

A	33	52	52	29	30	47
B	51	39	19	24	31	

Test, at the 10% level, the claim that the mean weekly telephone sales at Company A exceed those of Company B. State clearly any assumptions needed for your test to be valid.

Solution

The mean and variance for the two samples are as follows:

Sample	Size	Mean	Variance
A	6	40.5	100.92
B	5	32.8	128.16

Let X_1 and X_2 be the telephone sales for Companies A and B, respectively.

The assumptions needed to perform the test are given in Chapter 9:

- X_1 and X_2 both normally distributed;
- X_1 and X_2 have the same variance;
- the two samples are independent.

An unbiased estimate of the common variance is

$$S^2 = \frac{n_1 s_1^2 + n_2 s_2^2}{n_1 + n_2 - 2} = \frac{6 \times 100.92 + 5 \times 128.16}{6 + 5 - 2} = 138.48.$$

The hypotheses are $H_0: \mu_1 - \mu_2 = 0$ and $H_0: \mu_1 - \mu_2 > 0$.

Under H_0,

$$T = \frac{\overline{X}_1 - \overline{X}_2 - 0}{S\sqrt{\dfrac{1}{n_1} + \dfrac{1}{n_2}}}$$

follows the *t*-distribution with $v = n_1 + n_2 - 2$ degrees of freedom.

In this case, $v = 6 + 5 - 2 = 9$ so for a one-tailed test at the 10% level the critical region is $t > 1.383$.

The value of the test statistic is

$$t = \frac{40.5 - 32.8 - 0}{\sqrt{138.48\left(\frac{1}{6} + \frac{1}{5}\right)}} = 1.08.$$

This is not in the critical region, so we accept H_0.

At the 10% level there is insufficient evidence to support the claim that the mean telephone sales are higher for Company A.

Paired samples

Worked example

The first row of the table below shows the weekly number of telephone sales made by a random selection of five employees who work for an energy company.

The second row shows the sales of the same employees after they have been on a training course in customer relations.

Employee	A	B	C	D	E
Sales before training	57	32	37	41	36
Sales after training	56	36	43	49	43

Test, at the 5% level, whether the average sales have improved. State clearly any assumptions needed for your test to be valid.

Solution

This time the two samples are not independent. Instead the data is given in pairs: the figures in the two rows are the sales of the same five employees. If the numbers in either row were to be shuffled round the link would be broken, and some useful information would be lost. We are interested in the differences between numbers in each pair:

Employee	A	B	C	D	E
Difference	−1	4	6	8	7

The *t*-test can now be applied to this list provided that X, the random variable representing these differences, is normally distributed.

The sample mean and variance are checked easily; they are 4.8 and 10.16, respectively.

An unbiased estimate of the variance of X is

$$S^2 = \frac{5}{4} \times 10.16 = 12.7$$

so $S = 3.56$.

If μ denotes the mean of the population differences, the hypotheses are $H_0: \mu = 0$ and $H_1: \mu > 0$.

Under H_0,

$$\frac{\overline{X} - 0}{3.56/\sqrt{5}}$$

follows the *t*-distribution with $5 - 1 = 4$ degrees of freedom, so at the 5% level the critical region is $t > 2.132$. The value of the test statistic is

$$\frac{4.8 - 0}{3.56/\sqrt{5}} = 3.01.$$

This is in the critical region, so we reject H_0 in favour of H_1.

At the 5% level there is evidence to suggest that the mean sales have improved after the training programme (although whether this is solely attributable to the training or the result of other factors we cannot be certain).

Test yourself

Q3. Firms often use bank loans to finance their expansion. The top row of the table shows the amount of money (in £1,000s) lent to a random sample of small businesses.

After a period of quantitative easing (QE) from the Bank of England, a second random sample is taken and the amounts borrowed are given in the second row of the table.

Before QE	10	14	12	31	10	20	29
After QE	17	23	19	28	22	18	41

Test, at the 5% level, whether the average loan to small businesses has increased, assuming that the samples are

(a) independent;
(b) paired (that is, with each column representing money lent to the same firm).

In each case, state clearly all assumptions needed for the test to be valid.

Comment briefly on the conclusions from parts (a) and (b).

Errors

Key definitions

A **type I error** occurs when the null hypothesis, H_0, is rejected when it is, in fact, true.

A **type II error** occurs when the null hypothesis, H_0, is accepted when it is false (that is, when H_1 is true).

In hypothesis testing, we work on the basis that H_0 is true. We then decide to reject it when the sample mean is so extreme that it falls in the tail (or tails) of the normal (or t-) distribution defined in H_0. In effect, we say that the event of picking such a sample at random is so unlikely that there must be something wrong with H_0. However, it could be that H_0 really is true and that we have picked an extreme sample. For a 5% significance level, there is a 1 in 20 chance that this will happen, and that in rejecting H_0 we have actually made the wrong decision. This is a type I error and the probability that it occurs is just the significance level of the test (usually labelled α). To be specific, let us suppose that the rejection region is in the right-hand tail as illustrated in Figure 10.4.

Figure 10.5 also shows the distribution assuming that an alternative hypothesis, H_1, is true. The region to the left of the critical value corresponds to the values of the test statistic that lead to the decision to accept H_0. Therefore, the shaded area under the graph of H_1 gives the probability of accepting H_0 when H_1 is true. This is the probability of making a type II error and is usually written as β. In an ideal world, it would be good to minimise both errors. However, as Figure 10.5 indicates, this is impossible. As the critical value moves one way to reduce the size of one error, the other increases automatically.

Figure 10.6 shows the area under H_1 to the right of the critical value. This is the probability of rejecting H_0 correctly when H_1 is true. Given that the total area under H_1 is 1 this probability is $1 - \beta$. This number is called the *power of a hypothesis test*. If possible we try to design hypothesis tests to maximise this, while at the same time keeping α small.

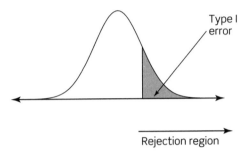

Figure 10.4

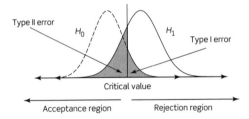

Figure 10.5

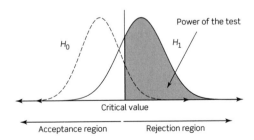

Figure 10.6

Worked example

The time (measured in worker-hours), X, for an accountancy firm to audit a company has a normal distribution with standard deviation 80 hours. A random sample of 10 audits is chosen. The mean times of the sample and population are $\bar{x}$ and μ, respectively. The null hypothesis $\mu = 500$ is tested against the alternative hypothesis, $\mu < 500$ at the 2.5% level.

(a) Find the range of values of $\bar{x}$ for which the null hypothesis is accepted.

(b) State the probability of making a type I error.

(c) Find the probability of making a type II error when $\mu = 425$, and deduce the power of the test.

Solution

(a) Under H_0,

$$\bar{X} \sim N\left(500, \frac{80^2}{10}\right)$$

and so

$$Z = \frac{\bar{X} - 500}{80/\sqrt{10}} - N(0, 1).$$

For a one-tailed test at the 2.5% level the critical region is $z < -1.96$.

The values of $\bar{x}$ that determine the acceptance region satisfy

$$\frac{\bar{x} - 500}{80/\sqrt{10}} > -1.96,$$

which rearranges as $\bar{x} > 450$.

(b) The probability of making a type I error is just the significance level, which is 0.025.

(c) Under H_1,

$$\bar{X} \sim N\left(425, \frac{80^2}{10}\right)$$

and so the probability that the null hypothesis is mistakenly accepted is $P(\bar{X} > 450) = P(Z > 0.988) = 0.1615$.

The probability of a type II error is 0.1615 and the power of the test is $1 - 0.1615 = 0.8385$.

Test yourself

Q4. Repeat the previous worked example, this time using a 10% significance level. Verify that increasing the type I error decreases the type II error.

Chapter summary – pulling it all together

By the end of this chapter you should be able to:

	Confident ✓	Not confident?
Use the normal distribution to perform a hypothesis test for a single mean or proportion		Revise pages 186–189
Use the normal distribution to perform a hypothesis test for the differences between two means or proportions		Revise pages 189–191
Perform a t-test for a single mean		Revise pages 191–192
Perform a t-test for the difference of two means distinguishing between paired and unpaired samples		Revise pages 193–196
Understand what is meant by a type I error, type II error and the power of a test		Revise pages 196–199

Now try the assessment question at the start of the chapter using the answer guidelines below.

Answer guidelines

✳ Assessment question

Prices of return flights to New York are normally distributed with standard deviation £100. An airline's advertising brochure claims that the average price is as low as £678. To test this claim a random sample of 20 flights are chosen, which give a mean price of £720.

(a) Test the airline's claim at the 5% level.

(b) What would the minimum significance level need to be to reject the null hypothesis for this particular sample?

(c) What assumptions or modifications (if any) would need to be made to the test when:

    (i) the population is not normal and a random sample of 50 flights is used;

    (ii) the population is normal but the standard deviation of the population is unknown and the sample size is 20.

(d) It is decided to investigate the hypotheses $H_0: \mu$ = £678 and $H_1: \mu$ = £720. Assuming that the flight prices are normally distributed with standard deviation £100, what sample size must be tested so that the probabilities of making a type I and type II error are 5% and 10%, respectively?

Approaching the question

- The first two parts of the question involve testing a single mean from a normal distribution. This can be done either using a rejection region or by calculating the p-value. Decide which method is easier for you.

- You are not expected to understand the mathematical analysis of the normal or t-distributions. However, you need to know the conditions under which the tests are valid. Make sure that you are aware of these before tackling part (c).

- Part (d) is not easy but highlights an important practical issue. As mentioned on page 197, there is a conflict between making both errors small at the same time. In this case you need to choose a sample size that ensures that both α and β are tolerable.

Method of solution

- The first part is a standard question requiring a standard response. Use the assessment advice on pages 184–185 as a checklist to make sure that you include all salient points.

  - If you choose to use the rejection region approach you will need to use the full normal tables to work out the probability in part (b).
  - If you choose to use the p-value approach then you can just state the answer to part (b) without any further work.

- In part (c) the examiner is checking that you are aware of the conditions under which the hypothesis tests are valid. Unfortunately there are quite a few variations on the theme and it can be difficult to identify the differences. The key point to remember is that whenever you know the sample variance instead of the population variance, you need to produce an unbiased estimate using the sample, and at the same time switch to the t-distribution, which is only valid when the parent population is normal.

- Part (d) is the most difficult part of the question. Figure 10.5 illustrates the situation. There are two unknowns in this question: the critical value of sample mean, $\bar{x}$, and the sample size, n. The aim is to use the information in the question to write down two equations. The key steps are as follows:

  - Assume that H_0 is true and write down the distribution of $\bar{X}$ in the usual way. For a one-tailed test at the 5% level, the critical value of z is -1.645. If you write down the standardised normal variable, Z, in terms of $\bar{X}$, it is possible to write down an equation involving the two unknowns, $\bar{x}$ and n.

  - Assume that H_1 is true, and write down the distribution of $\bar{X}$ in the usual way. The area under the H_1 graph to the right of the critical value in Figure 10.5 is given to be 0.1. From the normal tables the standardised variable, Z, is 1.282. If you write down the standardised normal variable, Z, in terms of $\bar{X}$, it is possible to write down an equation involving the two unknowns, $\bar{x}$ and n.

  - Finally, solve the simultaneous equations by eliminating $\bar{x}$ to find n.

Companion website

Go to the companion website at **www.pearsoned.co.uk/econexpress** to find more revision support online for this topic area.

Notes

11 Chi-squared distribution

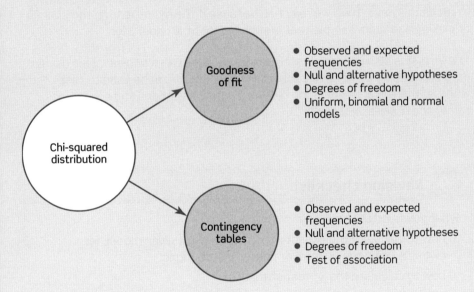

Introduction

The chi-squared distribution (written χ^2, pronounced kye-squared) is used to test whether a particular mathematical model fits a given data set. For example, a histogram of sample data might have a single hump that is fairly symmetric, thus leading us to suspect that the population follows a normal distribution. To test this suspicion, we would compare the actual data (the *observed frequencies*) with those predicted by the normal model (the *expected frequencies*). Provided that the two sets of frequencies are not too far apart, we then accept the normal distribution as a possible model.

The strategy is similar to that used in hypothesis testing, and we use the same notation and language. In this case the null hypothesis, H_0, states that the data can be modelled by the normal distribution; the alternative hypothesis states that this is not a suitable model. We select a significance level, which is usually 5%, and calculate a certain test statistic, which measures how far apart the observed and expected frequencies are. This is then compared with a critical value, found from the χ^2 tables. If our test statistic exceeds this value then we reject H_0 because if the model is true, the chance of picking a random sample that is such a poor fit is under 5%.

The χ^2 test is also used for testing association between two variables using data provided by contingency tables. For example, it can be used to test whether there is an association between voting intentions and social class, salary and IT skills, and so on.

Revision checklist

What you need to know:
- ❏ how to calculate the expected frequencies in a given model, for example using the uniform or normal distributions;
- ❏ how to calculate the χ^2 test statistic;
- ❏ what is meant by the phrase "degrees of freedom", and how to find this number;
- ❏ how to perform the hypothesis test that a particular distribution provides a good model for a data set;
- ❏ how to calculate the expected frequencies in a contingency table;
- ❏ how to perform a hypothesis test for association between two variables.

Assessment advice

Use the following six-step strategy when testing the goodness of fit of a model:

- State the null and alternative hypotheses. The null hypothesis, H_0, states that the model is true; the alternative hypothesis, H_1, states that it is not true.
- Calculate the expected frequencies assuming that the model is true. If any of these values are less than five then combine some adjacent cells together.
- Work out the number of degrees of freedom, which is the number of cells minus the number of restrictions.
- Look up the critical value of χ^2 in statistical tables.
- Calculate the test statistic,

$$\chi^2 = \sum \frac{(O - E)^2}{E},$$

where O and E are the observed and expected frequencies.
- State the conclusion of the test, including the significance level. If the value of the test statistic exceeds the critical value, reject H_0; otherwise, accept H_0.

Assessment question

Could you answer this question? Guidelines on answering the question are presented at the end of this chapter.

(a)   A large engineering firm employs graduates in four departments: Human Resources, Marketing & Sales, IT & Technical Support, and Research & Development.

The data for a random sample of 120 graduates employed by the company are shown in Table 11.1. Across the whole company, the number of staff employed in these departments is in the ratio 1:2:3:4.

(i)   Test, at the 5% level, whether this ratio could apply to all graduate employees.

(ii)   Do you think that the 1:2:3:4 model is suggested by the figures in Table 11.1?

(iii) Explain any apparent discrepancy between your answers to (i) and (ii).

Table 11.1

Human Resources	Marketing & Sales	IT & Technical Support	Research & Development
17	30	33	40

(b)   The salaries of these 120 graduates are shown in Table 11.2. Test, at the 5% level, the company's claim that there is no association between gender and salary.

Table 11.2

Salary	£20,000 to £30,000	£30,001 to £40,000	£40,001 and above	Total
Men	25	38	25	88
Women	6	10	16	32
Total	31	48	41	120

Goodness of fit

To motivate the general strategy, we begin with a simple example. Suppose that a single die is rolled 120 times and that the scores shown in Table 11.3 are obtained.

If the die is unbiased, then we can model this situation using the uniform distribution and we would expect to get equal numbers of each score as shown in Table 11.4.

It would, of course, be wrong to expect to have rolled exactly equal numbers. However, if the die really is unbiased, then the figures in Tables 11.3 and 11.4 should be reasonably close.

Table 11.3

Score	1	2	3	4	5	6
Observed frequency, O	15	21	29	16	14	25

Table 11.4

Score	1	2	3	4	5	6
Expected frequency, E	20	20	20	20	20	20

Key definition

If O and E denote the observed and expected frequencies, then the **test statistic,**

$$x^2 = \sum \frac{(O - E)^2}{E},$$

provides a measure of how well the model fits the data.

The numbers $O - E$ are the differences between the observed and expected values, which are squared to make them positive. These are divided by the expected frequency, E, and summed to give the total. The reason for dividing each term by E is to make sure that the relative sizes of the data items are taken into account. For example, a difference of 7 in the value 120 is less significant than a difference of 3 in the value 12. Division by E creates a level playing field in which each disparity is fairly represented.

From Tables 11.3 and 11.4,

$$X^2 = \frac{(15 - 20)^2}{20} + \frac{(21 - 20)^2}{20} + \frac{(29 - 20)^2}{20}$$

$$+ \frac{(16 - 20)^2}{20} + \frac{(14 - 20)^2}{20} + \frac{(25 - 20)^2}{20} = 9.2.$$

The test statistic is now compared with the critical value obtained from the χ^2 tables. These tables depend on two things: the significance level and the number of degrees of freedom. The first of these is specified in advance by the user of the test, and the second needs to be worked out. A typical significance level is 5%. To work out the number of degrees of freedom in this example, imagine being allowed to invent a set of numbers to go in the six cells in Table 11.3. Once the first five cells have been allocated a value, the last cell must be chosen so that the total number adds up to 120, because this is the figure that we used to work out the expected frequencies in Table 11.4. In practice, therefore, we are only free to choose numbers to go into five of the six cells.

> ### Key definition
>
> The **number of degrees of freedom** is the number of cells minus the number of restrictions.

In this case there are six cells and one restriction, giving five degrees of freedom.

Table 11.5 gives an extract from the x^2 distribution tables. The critical value at the 5% level, when there are five degrees of freedom, is 11.1. The critical region consists of all values greater than this. For this example, we reject H_0 when the test statistic exceeds 11.1. In fact, it is only 9.2 so is not in the critical region. Therefore, we accept the uniform distribution as a possible model and conclude that there is no evidence at the 5% level to suggest that the die is biased.

The general strategy was given in the assessment advice at the beginning of this chapter, and is summarised below:

> 1 State the null and alternative hypotheses.
> 2 Calculate the expected frequencies. If any of these values are less than 5, combine the cells.
> 3 Work out the number of degrees of freedom.
> 4 Look up the critical value of x^2 in statistical tables.
> 5 Calculate the test statistic,
>
> $$x^2 = \sum \frac{(O - E)^2}{E}.$$
>
> 6 State the conclusion of the test.

Table 11.5

Degrees of freedom	0.250	0.100	0.050	0.025	0.010	0.005	0.001
1	1.32	2.71	3.84	5.02	6.63	7.88	10.8
2	2.77	4.61	5.99	7.38	9.21	10.6	13.8
3	4.11	6.25	7.81	9.35	11.3	12.8	16.3
4	5.39	7.78	9.49	11.1	13.3	14.9	18.5
5	6.63	9.24	11.1	12.8	15.1	16.7	20.5
6	7.84	10.6	12.6	14.4	16.8	18.5	22.5

Worked example

The ages of a random sample of 100 employees in a firm are shown on Table 11.6. Test the hypothesis that the parent population is normally distributed.

Table 11.6

Age	18–24	25–34	35–44	45–54	55–64	Over 64
Observed frequency	5	11	33	28	16	7

Solution

Before we begin the χ^2 test there are two observations to make about this data set. Firstly note that in western cultures, someone claiming to be 34 years of age would do so up to midnight on the day before their 35th birthday, so the group 25–34 actually goes from 25 to 35. Secondly, recall that the normal distribution itself goes on forever at the two ends, running from $-\infty$ to $+\infty$, so when working out the expected frequencies, the first group goes from $-\infty$ to 25 and the last group covers people aged from 65 to ∞. This may seem strange because children (including those with negative ages!) and people aged over 100 do not work. However, in practice the area under the extreme sections of the normal curve is so small, that it doesn't actually contribute significantly to the expected frequencies. This is illustrated in Figure 11.1.

The normal distribution, $N(\mu, \sigma^2)$, involves two parameters, μ and σ^2, that are not given in the question so must be found from the data set. Chapter 9 shows how to calculate unbiased estimates of the mean and variance. You might like to use Table 11.6 to check for yourself that these are 46.08 and 147.68, respectively, where the midpoint of the last group was estimated to be 70.

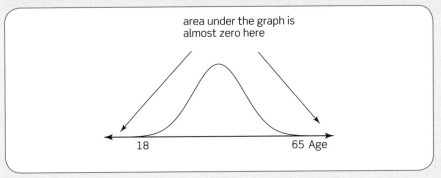

Figure 11.1

Step 1

The null hypothesis, H_0, is that the parent population follows the $N(46.08, 147.68)$ distribution; the alternative hypothesis, H_1, is that it does not follow this distribution.

Step 2

The standardised variable is

$$Z = \frac{X - 46.08}{\sqrt{147.68}} \sim N(0, 1),$$

where X is the random variable of ages in the firm.

The probability that someone is in the first group is given by

$$P(X < 25) = P\left(Z < \frac{25 - 46.08}{\sqrt{147.68}}\right) = P(Z < -1.735) = 0.0414.$$

There are 100 employees in the sample, so to convert probabilities to expected frequencies we multiply by 100. According to the normal model, there are 4.14 employees aged under 25 in the firm.

The probability that someone is in the second group is given by

$$P(25 \leq X < 35) = P\left(\frac{25 - 46.08}{\sqrt{147.68}} \leq Z < \frac{35 - 46.08}{\sqrt{147.68}}\right)$$
$$= P(-1.735 \leq Z < -0.912) = 0.1395,$$

so the expected frequency is 13.95. The complete set of expected frequencies is shown in Table 11.7.

Unfortunately, the χ^2 test can only be used when the expected frequencies exceed 5. In this case the expected frequency in the first cell is less than 5 so we must avoid this by merging the first two cells, as shown in Table 11.8.

Table 11.7

Age	18–24	25–34	35–44	45–54	55–64	Over 64
Expected frequency	4.14	13.95	28.36	30.40	17.17	5.98

Step 3

When working out the expected frequencies we used three facts from the observed frequency table (total, mean and variance), so three constraints are imposed on the five cells. The number of degrees of freedom is 5 − 3 = 2.

Step 4

At the 5% level, with two degrees of freedom, Table 11.5 shows that the critical value of X^2 is 5.99.

Step 5

$$X^2 = \frac{(16 - 18.09)^2}{18.09} + \frac{(33 - 28.36)^2}{28.36} + \frac{(28 - 30.40)^2}{30.40}$$

$$+ \frac{(16 - 17.17)^2}{17.17} + \frac{(7 - 5.98)^2}{5.98} = 1.44,$$

which is less than the critical value.

Step 6

At the 5% level, there is evidence to suggest that this normal distribution is a good fit of the data.

In this example neither the mean nor the variance was given, so we had to work them out from the observed frequency table. However, had these two statistics been supplied externally, it would not have been necessary for the data in Table 11.7 to have these particular mean and variance values. Under these circumstances the only constraint on the observed frequencies is the total, so the number of degrees of freedom would have been 5 − 1 = 4.

Table 11.8

Age	18-34	35-44	45-54	55-64	Over 64
Observed frequencies	16	33	28	16	7
Expected frequencies	18.09	28.36	30.40	17.17	5.98

Test yourself

Q1. The number of days of sick leave that a random sample of 100 employees experienced during 30 consecutive days is shown in Table 11.9. It is decided to use this data to test the hypothesis that the number of days' sick leave that an employee takes in a 30-day period can be modelled by a binomial distribution, $B(30, p)$.

Table 11.9

Number of days off work	0	1	2	3	4	5
Number of employees	21	27	23	21	7	1

(a) Calculate the mean of this data set and deduce that an estimate for p is given by 0.0563.

(b) Test, at the 5% level, the hypothesis that the number of days can be modelled by the $B(30, 0.0563)$ distribution. Comment on your conclusion.

Contingency tables

Two-way tables, known as *contingency tables*, display data involving two variables. The χ^2 distribution can be used to test whether or not there is an association between the two variables.

Table 11.10 shows the degree classification awarded to a random sample of 300 students at three institutions, labelled A, B and C. One interesting question to ask about this data is whether there is any association between the degree classification and institution. For example, are you less likely to be awarded a

Table 11.10

	First	Upper second	Lower second	Third	Total
A	35	35	15	15	100
B	20	50	30	20	120
C	20	20	28	12	80
Total	75	105	73	47	300

first-class degree if you study at institution B? The figures seem to suggest that might be true but this could just be a feature of this particular sample, and we might not be justified in making such a claim for the whole population.

In order to analyse this information properly, we work out the table of expected frequencies based on the assumption that there is no association, and then perform a χ^2 test on the differences between the observed and expected frequencies. The procedure is the same as before.

Step 1

The null hypothesis, H_0, is that there is no association between degree classification and institution; the alternative hypothesis, H_1, is that there is an association.

Step 2

If H_0 is true then the probability of someone being awarded a first-class degree is independent of the institution. Therefore, the probability that someone chosen at random gets a first-class degree *and* studies at institution A can be found by multiplying these two separate probabilities together. The probability that someone is awarded a first is $75 \div 300$, because Table 11.10 shows that 75 firsts are awarded to the 300 students. It also shows that the probability that someone studies at institution A is $100/300$. By the multiplication law for independent events,

$$P \text{ (first class degree and studies at A)} = \frac{75}{300} \times \frac{100}{300}.$$

To convert probabilities into expected frequencies we multiply by 300, so the expected number of students awarded first-class degrees from institution A is

$$\frac{75}{300} \times \frac{100}{300} \times 300 = \frac{75 \times 100}{300}.$$

Notice that the numbers on the top of this fraction are the respective row and column totals, and the number on the bottom is the grand total of all the students in the sample.

Key definition

The **expected frequencies** in a contingency table are worked out from

$$\frac{\text{(row total)} \times \text{(column total)}}{\text{grand total}}.$$

The complete table of expected frequencies is shown in Table 11.11.

Table 11.11

	First	Upper second	Lower second	Third	Total
A	25	35	24.33	15.67	100
B	30	42	29.2	18.8	120
C	20	28	19.47	12.53	80
Total	75	105	73	47	300

Table 11.12

	First	Upper second	Lower second	Third	Total
A	X	X	X		100
B	X	X	X		120
C					80
Total	75	105	73	47	300

Step 3

To work out the number of degrees of freedom, imagine being allowed to fill in the table of observed frequencies and that you have reached the stage shown in Table 11.12, where the X indicates that you have already chosen which number to place in this cell.

The empty cells in the table can now be filled in by making sure that the row and column totals equal those in the table. In this case we are free to complete all but the last row and column in the table, and see that the number of degrees of freedom is $2 \times 3 = 6$.

Key definition

The **number of degrees of freedom** in a contingency table with *m* rows and *n* columns (ignoring the total rows and columns) is $(m - 1) \times (n - 1)$.

Table 11.13

	First	Upper second	Lower second	Third
A	4	0	3.58	0.03
B	3.33	1.52	0.02	0.08
C	0	2.29	3.74	0.02

Step 4

At the 5% level, with six degrees of freedom, the critical value is 12.6.

Step 5

Table 11.13 shows the contribution of each cell to the test statistic,

$$X^2 = \sum \frac{(O - E)^2}{E},$$

with a total of 18.6.

Step 6

This exceeds the critical value, so we reject H_0. At the 5% level we conclude that there is evidence of an association between degree classification and institutions. Table 11.13 enables us to analyse this more closely. The cells that make the largest contribution to the total highlight particular areas where further investigation might be useful. For example the awarding of third-class degrees is consistent across all three institutions, whereas the awarding of first-class degrees is an area of concern.

Test yourself

Q2. A random sample of 200 people in a small town was asked whether or not they passed their recent driving test, and which examiner they were given. Their responses are shown in Table 11.14. Test, at the 5% level, the claim that success in your driving test depends on which examiner you are allocated.

Table 11.14

Examiner	A	B	C
Pass	52	34	60
Fail	12	22	20

Chapter summary – pulling it all together

By the end of this chapter you should be able to:

	Confident ✓	Not confident?
Test for the goodness of fit of the uniform distribution		Revise pages 206–208
Test for the goodness of fit of the normal distribution		Revise pages 209–211
Test for association in a contingency table		Revise pages 212–215

Now try the assessment question at the start of the chapter using the answer guidelines below.

Answer guidelines

✱ Assessment question

(a) A large engineering firm employs graduates in four departments: Human Resources, Marketing & Sales, IT & Technical Support, and Research & Development.

The data for a random sample of 120 graduates employed by the company are shown in Table 11.1. Across the whole company, the number of staff employed in these departments is in the ratio 1:2:3:4.

(i) Test, at the 5% level, whether this ratio could apply to all graduate employees.

(ii) Do you think that the 1:2:3:4 model is suggested by the figures in Table 11.1?

Table 11.1

Human Resources	Marketing & Sales	IT &Technical Support	Research & Development
17	30	33	40

(iii) Explain any apparent discrepancy between your answers to (i) and (ii).

(b)   The salaries of these 120 graduates are shown in Table 11.2. Test, at the 5% level, the company's claim that there is no association between gender and salary.

Table 11.2

Salary	£20,000 to £30,000	£30,001 to £40,000	£40,001 and above	Total
Men	25	38	25	88
Women	6	10	16	32
Total	31	48	41	120

Approaching the question

- There are two parts to this question that are independent of each other.

- In both parts, use the six-point strategy given in the Assessment Advice on page 205.

- Part (b) is a standard question very similar to that given on page 212.

Method of solution

- In part (a) follow the six-step strategy:
  - The null and alternative hypotheses are easy to state.
  - The numbers 1, 2, 3 and 4 in the ratio add up to 10. So if the model is true, then one-tenth of graduate employees work in HR, two-tenths work in Marketing, and so on. The only restriction on the data is that it adds up to 120.
  - Common mistakes when working out the test statistic are to divide by the observed frequencies, instead of the expected frequencies, and to perform the division before squaring.
  - Do not forget to mention the significance level in your conclusion.

- The last two parts of the question provide you with an opportunity to analyse the χ^2 test critically. If you were presented with Table 11.1 on its own, would the 1:2:3:4 model really suggest itself? What feature of the methodology in the test has led to the apparent acceptance of the model?

- In part (b) follow the six-step strategy:
  - The null and alternative hypotheses are easy to state.
  - Copy out the table for the observed frequencies, putting in an extra row and column for the totals. The formula for the expected frequencies is

    $$\frac{\text{(row total)} \times \text{(column total)}}{\text{grand total}}.$$

  - You do not need to explain where this formula comes from unless asked to do so. Just use it to produce a table of expected frequencies. As a check, make sure that the row and column totals have not changed.

  - The formula $(m - 1) \times (n - 1)$ can be used to work out the number of degrees of freedom, where m and n are the number of rows and columns.

  - It is always tempting just to work out the test statistic in one go on a calculator and write the final value down. Unfortunately, if you make a mistake you cannot be awarded any marks: it is better to play safe and at least write the working down for each cell.

  - As usual, don't forget to mention the significance level in your conclusion.

Companion website

Go to the companion website at **www.pearsoned.co.uk/econexpress** to find more revision support online for this topic area.

Notes

Notes

12 Correlation and regression

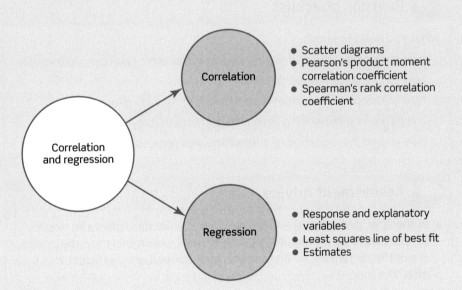

- **Correlation**
  - Scatter diagrams
  - Pearson's product moment correlation coefficient
  - Spearman's rank correlation coefficient

- **Correlation and regression**

- **Regression**
  - Response and explanatory variables
  - Least squares line of best fit
  - Estimates

A printable version of this topic map is available from **www.pearsoned.co.uk/econexpress**

Introduction

In economics we are often interested in whether or not two (or more) variables are related in some way. Perhaps the rate of inflation is related to the money supply, or a country's balance of payments might be connected to growth. The simplest way of detecting a possible correlation is to plot points on a scatter diagram. This will show whether or not:

- there is a tendency for one variable to increase or decrease as the other increases;
- the data points lie close to a straight line (*linear correlation*).

In this chapter we express this qualitative behaviour more precisely using statistics. Spearman's rank correlation coefficient measures the first property, and Pearson's product moment correlation coefficient (PMCC) is used to test for any linearity of the relationship. If there is a linear correlation, then it is possible to find a mathematical equation for the line of best fit, which can then be used to interpolate the data points and make predictions.

 ## Revision checklist

What you need to know:
- ❏ how to describe the correlation shown in a scatter diagram qualitatively;
- ❏ how to calculate Pearson's PMCC;
- ❏ how to calculate Spearman's coefficient of rank correlation;
- ❏ the difference between a response and explanatory variable;
- ❏ how to find the equation of a least squares regression line.

✳ Assessment advice

- Remember that when the PMCC is +1 (or −1) the data points lie exactly on an upward (or downward) sloping straight line. In this case the points are perfectly ranked, so Spearman's rank correlation coefficient must also be +1 (or −1).

- Remember that when Spearman's rank correlation coefficient is +1 (or −1) the data points are perfectly ranked. However, the points don't have to lie on a straight line for this to be true, so the value of the PMCC may not be +1 (or −1).

- Make sure that you can work out both the correlation coefficient and regression line using any summary data provided, as well as using the facilities available on your calculator.

- Remember that the estimates obtained from a regression line may be unreliable whenever:
  - the value of PMCC is not near ±1;
  - the value of the explanatory variable is towards the end of (or outside) the range of available data points;
  - the number of data points is small.

✱ Assessment question

Could you answer this question? Guidelines on answering the question are presented at the end of this chapter.

Table 12.1 shows a product's monthly advertising expenditure, A, and the corresponding sales revenue, S, for a random sample of 12 months.

Table 12.1

A (£100s)	5	26	16	20	35	0	22	10	13	19	14	9
S (£1,000s)	11	32	20	25	33	2	26	12	17	27	16	13

[Summary data:

$$\sum A_i = 189, \ \sum S_i = 234, \ \sum A_i S_i = 4629, \ \sum A_i^2 = 3973, \ \sum S_i^2 = 5526]$$

(a) Calculate the sample correlation coefficient, and give a brief interpretation of its value.

(b) Identify the explanatory variable, and find the equation of the line of best fit.

(c) Estimate sales in a month when advertising expenditure is £3,300, and comment on the reliability of this estimate.

(d) Draw a scatter diagram together with the line of best fit. Describe briefly, in qualitative terms, an improved model for this data set.

Correlation

Table 12.2 shows the 2010 GDP per capita of nine countries. (This is gross domestic product divided by the mid-year population, and is measured in US dollars.) The table also shows the life expectancy at birth in each country.

This indicates the number of years a child born in 2010 would live if prevailing patterns of mortality were to stay the same throughout its life. A scatter diagram representing this data is plotted in Figure 12.1; it indicates that children born in countries with higher levels of GDP per capita tend to have higher levels of life expectancy and vice versa.

Table 12.2

Country	GDP per capita in 2010* ($)	Life expectancy in 2010* (years)
Australia	50,746	82
Brazil	10,993	73
Cyprus	28,779	79
Estonia	14,045	75
Germany	39,852	80
India	1,375	65
Malaysia	8,373	74
Namibia	4,876	62
Russian Federation	10,481	69

*Source: World Bank, http://data.worldbank.org.

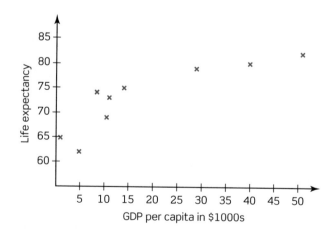

Figure 12.1

The diagram also suggests a possible linear relationship between the two variables. There is a fairly strong positive correlation between life expectancy and GDP per capita. We use the phrase "fairly strong" because the points lie quite close to a straight line, and use the word "positive" because this line slopes uphill.

It is tempting to claim that this scatter diagram proves that high life expectancy is due to high levels of GDP per capita. While there may be some truth in this, in general we must be cautious about any statements that we make. In this example, there is no indication about why these particular nine countries were chosen. Even if they were selected at random, the sample size is too small to be certain that this correlation extends to the rest of the world.

In addition, if there is a strong correlation between two variables, we cannot always claim that this relation is necessarily one of cause and effect. To understand this, imagine that the general shape of Figure 12.1 represents a scatter diagram of road accidents plotted against the number of takeaway restaurants in nine towns in the UK. It would be ludicrous to blame the presence of a large number of takeaways for the high number of road accidents in a town. In this case, a town with a large number of restaurants is likely to have a high population, which in turn is likely to produce a relatively large number of accidents.

Figure 12.2 shows other scatter diagrams, together with the phrases that could be used to describe their correlation. These phrases are certainly sensible but are far too vague and subjective to be of any use. Instead we prefer to calculate numerical statistics, which provide a more objective measure. The two most widely used statistics are:

- Pearson's product moment correlation coefficient;
- Spearman's rank correlation coefficient.

We consider each of these in turn.

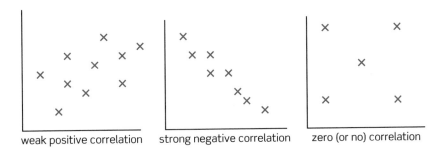

weak positive correlation   strong negative correlation   zero (or no) correlation

Figure 12.2

Pearson's product moment correlation coefficient

Key definition

If the n data points on a scatter diagram are denoted by (x_i, y_i) then **Pearson's product moment correlation** is given by

$$r = \frac{S_{xy}}{\sqrt{S_{xx} S_{yy}}}$$

where

$$S_{xy} = \sum x_i y_i - \frac{\sum x_i \sum y_i}{n},$$

$$S_{xx} = \sum x_i^2 - \frac{(\sum x_i)^2}{n},$$

$$S_{yy} = \sum y_i^2 - \frac{(\sum y_i)^2}{n}.$$

The PMCC is often called the "sample correlation coefficient" or just "correlation coefficient". It measures linear correlation and has the following properties:

- It always lies between −1 and +1. If your value lies outside this range then you have made a mistake.
- If $r = +1$ then the data points have perfect positive correlation, which means that the points lie exactly on an upwards-sloping straight line.
- If $r = -1$ then the data points have perfect negative correlation, which means that the points lie exactly on a downward-sloping straight line.
- If $r = 0$ there is no correlation (although in practice most data sets have at least some correlation so a value of exactly zero is unlikely to occur).
- The value of r has no units and is independent of the choice of scale on the axes of a scatter diagram.

Worked example

Find the value of the correlation coefficient for the bivariate data given in Table 12.1.

Solution

To avoid very big numbers we will divide all of the values of GDP per capita by 1,000. As noted in the last property, this does not affect the value of r.

It is easy to check that

$$\sum x_i = 169.52, \quad \sum y_i = 659, \quad \sum x_i y_i = 13{,}213.215,$$

$$\sum x_i^2 = 5{,}515.301826, \quad \sum y_i^2 = 48{,}625$$

so

$$S_{xy} = \sum x_i y_i - \frac{\sum x_i \sum y_i}{n} = 13{,}213.215 - \frac{169.52 \times 659}{9} = 800.584;$$

$$S_{xx} = \sum x_i^2 - \frac{(\sum x_i)^2}{n} = 5{,}515.301826 - \frac{169.52^2}{9} = 2322.298;$$

$$S_{yy} = \sum y_i^2 - \frac{(\sum y_i)^2}{n} = 48{,}625 - \frac{659^2}{9} = 371.556;$$

$$r = \frac{S_{xy}}{\sqrt{S_{xx} S_{yy}}} = \frac{800.584}{\sqrt{2322.298 \times 371.556}} = 0.862.$$

The value of r is reasonably close to $+1$, confirming that there is fairly strong positive correlation.

Test yourself

Q1. A firm is planning to launch a new product but is uncertain about what price, x (in £s), to charge. Market research estimates possible sales, y (£1,000s), at various key price points, as shown in Table 12.3.

Table 12.3

Price	24	35	30	14	20	50	38
Sales	29	22	25	44	31	18	21

[Summary data:

$$\sum x_i = 211, \quad \sum y_i = 190, \quad \sum x_i y_i = 5150, \quad \sum x_i^2 = 7241, \quad \sum y_i^2 = 5612]$$

(a) Calculate the correlation coefficient and give a brief interpretation of this value.

(b) Draw the scatter diagram and hence describe, in qualitative terms, how sales vary with price.

It is possible to perform a significance test on the value of r using the t-distribution, although this is beyond the scope of this book. However, you should be aware that the importance of the value of r depends on the size of the sample. A correlation coefficient of 0.4 based on a sample of 10,000 data points may well be more significant than a correlation coefficient of 0.7 based on a sample of just 10 points.

Spearman's rank correlation coefficient

Figure 12.3 presents two scatter diagrams in which the points show a strong relationship that is non-linear. The relationship in Figure 12.3(a) is perfectly ranked. It could well be quadratic or exponential but this will not be picked up using the PMCC, which only identifies linear correlation. The relationship in Figure 12.3(b) is more complicated but the diagram displays points that are perfectly ranked in reverse order: the point with the highest x coordinate has the lowest y coordinate, the point with the second-highest x coordinate has the second lowest y coordinate, and so on.

Spearman's rank correlation coefficient measures the amount of agreement in the ranks of a data set. It could be worked out by substituting the ranks into the formula for the PMCC. However, *provided there are no tied ranks,* a simpler formula can be used.

> **Key definition**
>
> **Spearman's rank correlation coefficient** is given by
>
> $$\rho = 1 - \frac{6 \sum d_i^2}{n(n^2 - 1)}$$
>
> where n = the number of data points and d_i = difference in the ranks of the ith data point.

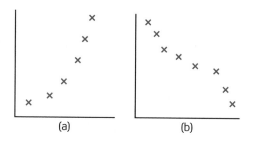

(a)   (b)

Figure 12.3

It has the following properties:

- It always lies between −1 and +1. If your value lies outside this range then you have made a mistake.
- If $\rho = +1$ then both rank orders are identical (Figure 12.3a).
- If $\rho = -1$ then one rank order is the exact reverse of the other (Figure 12.3b).
- If ρ is close to zero then there is little agreement between the two rank orders.

Worked example

Find the value of Spearman's rank correlation coefficient for the data given in Table 12.2.

Solution

The ranks for each country are listed in Table 12.4. The fourth column gives the square of the differences in the ranks, which has a total of 8.

Table 12.4

Country	GDP per capita rankings	Life expectancy rankings	d_i^2
Australia	1	1	0
Brazil	5	6	1
Cyprus	3	3	0
Estonia	4	4	0
Germany	2	2	0
India	9	8	1
Malaysia	7	5	4
Namibia	8	9	1
Russian Federation	6	7	1
Total			8

$$\rho = 1 - \frac{6\sum d_i^2}{n(n^2 - 1)} = 1 - \frac{6 \times 8}{9 \times 80} = \frac{14}{15}.$$

This value is close to +1, indicating a strong level of agreement between the ranks.

Regression

We mentioned in the previous section that sometimes one of the variables *depends* on the other variable. If there is an implied direction of causality then we usually plot the dependent variable on the vertical axis and the independent variable on the horizontal axis. For the worked example considered previously, if there is a causality relationship then it must be that life expectancy depends on GDP per capita, not the other way around. Life expectancy is therefore the *response* variable and GDP per capita is the *explanatory* variable. The explanatory variable is sometimes called the *controlled* variable. For the previous Test Yourself question, the price is clearly being controlled and the sales depend on these values, which is why prices are plotted on the horizontal axis and sales on the vertical axis.

Sometimes neither variable is controlled. In these circumstances the use of the line of best fit dictates which variable is chosen as the explanatory variable. If a table of paired values is provided for variables labelled S and W, say, and you want to use a regression line to predict values of S from given values of W, then W is the explanatory variable. The scatter diagram is plotted with W on the horizontal axis and S on the vertical axis.

Figure 12.4 shows a scatter diagram together with a straight line, which is one of many possible lines that pass close to the data points. The x coordinate of each data point is assumed to be exact because this variable is controlled. However, values taken by the response variable are inexact: the relationship

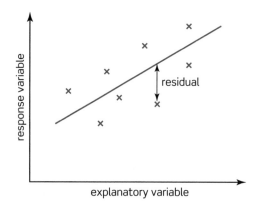

Figure 12.4

is not exactly linear, and may well be subject to the influence of other factors that may vary randomly. The vertical distance from the line to each data point is called the *error* or *residual*.

Key definitions

The **line of best fit** is the one that minimises the sum of the squares of the residuals and is sometimes called the **least squares regression line y on x.** The equation of this line is given by $y = a + bx$, where

$$b = \frac{S_{xy}}{S_{xx}}$$

and $a = \bar{y} - b\bar{x}$.

The gradient is given by

$$\frac{S_{xy}}{S_{xx}}$$

and the condition, $a = \bar{y} - b\bar{x}$, states that the line of best fit passes through the mean point $(\bar{x}, \bar{y})$.

Worked example

(a) Find the line of best fit for the bivariate data given in Table 12.2.

(b) In 2010, the GDP per capita in the UK was \$36,186. Estimate the life expectancy of an infant born in the UK in 2010, and comment on the reliability of this estimate.

Solution

(a) As in the previous worked example, we let the x coordinate be measured in thousands of US\$. The values of S_{xy} and S_{xx} have already been calculated to be 800.584 and 2,322.298, respectively. The coordinates of the mean point are given by

$$\bar{x} = \frac{\sum x_i}{n} = \frac{169.52}{9} = 18.836$$

and

$$\bar{y} = \frac{\sum y_i}{n} = \frac{659}{9} = 73.222.$$

Hence the line of best fit is given by $y = a + bx$ where

$$b = \frac{S_{xy}}{S_{xx}} = \frac{800.584}{2322.298} = 0.345$$

and $a = \bar{y} - b\bar{x} = 73.222 - 0.345 \times 18.836 = 66.729.$

The equation is $y = 66.729 + 0.345x$; this is shown on the scatter diagram in Figure 12.5.

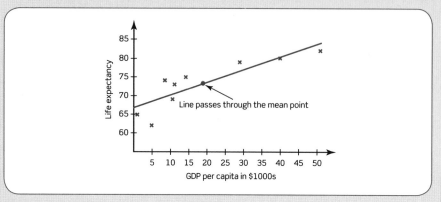

Figure 12.5

(b) Substituting $x = 36.186$ gives $y = 66.729 + 0.345 \times 36.186 = 79.$

The model predicts that someone born in the UK in 2010 can expect to live for 79 years. One might expect that this is a reasonable estimate because the PMCC for this data set was found to be 0.862, which is close to +1, and the value of the explanatory variable for the UK was within the range of values supplied. The only concern is that the sample size was quite small and may not have been random. In fact, the true value of life expectancy for the UK in 2010 was 80 so this model has produced a good estimate in this case.

Test yourself

Q3. For the data in Table 12.3 (Test Yourself Q1):

   (a) Find the line of best fit.

   (b) Hence estimate the sales when the price is (i) £10 and (ii) £27.

   (c) Comment on the reliability of the estimates in part (b).

Chapter summary – pulling it all together

By the end of this chapter you should be able to:

	Confident ✓	Not confident?
Describe the correlation qualitatively using a scatter diagram		Revise pages 224–225
Work out the value of the product moment correlation coefficient		Revise pages 226–227
Work out the value of Spearman's rank correlation coefficient		Revise pages 228–229
Find a line of best fit		Revise pages 230–232

Now try the assessment question at the start of the chapter using the answer guidelines below.

Answer guidelines

✱ Assessment question

Table 12.1 shows a product's monthly advertising expenditure, A, and the corresponding sales revenue, S, for a random sample of 12 months.

Table 12.1

A (£100s)	5	26	16	20	35	0	22	10	13	19	14	9
S (£1,000s)	11	32	20	25	33	2	26	12	17	27	16	13

[Summary data:

$\sum A_i = 189$, $\sum S_i = 234$, $\sum A_i S_i = 4629$, $\sum A_i^2 = 3973$,

$\sum S_i^2 = 5526$]

(a) Calculate the sample correlation coefficient, and give a brief interpretation of its value.

(b) Identify the explanatory variable, and find the equation of the line of best fit.

(c) Estimate sales in a month when advertising expenditure is £3,300, and comment on the reliability of this estimate.

(d) Draw a scatter diagram together with the line of best fit. Describe briefly, in qualitative terms, an improved model for this data set.

Approaching the question

- This question is in four parts. You need the regression line in part (b) to work out the estimate in part (c) but the remaining parts are fairly independent of each other.

- If you are proficient at using the correlation and regression routines on your calculator, you may prefer to just enter the data pairs directly into your machine when tackling the first two parts. However, be aware that if you do this and make a mistake, you are in danger of losing all the marks for the calculations.

- Most of the marks in part (c) are likely to be awarded for your comments rather than for the calculation.

- In part (d) you need to do two things. First, put the line of best fit on your scatter diagram. Also, there may be other features in the detail of the scatter diagram that you notice. Write these down and try to explain them in context if you can.

Method of solution

- You have been given the summary data in this question as well as the original. Therefore, it would be sensible to use this information to work out the value of r using the formula given on page 226. The worked example on page 227 shows how to do this. If you have the time in an exam, you could always check your answer using the specialised calculator functions.

- Don't forget to interpret your answer to part (a). This is your chance to explain that you appreciate that r is between -1 and $+1$, and that as r approaches these extremes the points get ever closer to a straight line. Try to put your remarks in context to score high marks.

- It is obvious what the explanatory variable is in part (b) but rather than just stating the answer, give a reason. This is your opportunity to convince the examiner that you know the difference between an explanatory and a response variable.

- The calculation of the line of best fit is standard. A worked example is given on page 231. Don't forget to reuse some of the working in part (a).

- Using a regression line to predict values in part (c) is straightforward. However, make sure that you comment on the reliability of this estimate in detail. The assessment advice on page 223 lists three things that you should consider.

- The line of best fit can be drawn through the y-intercept (which is the value of *a*) and the mean point. The correlation coefficient is a good way of measuring the extent to which a straight line that passes close to all the data points can be found across the entire range. However, it is not so good at picking out other trends or local features of a data set. The last part of the question is designed to encourage you to identify these and to explain them in context if you can. Look carefully at the two ends of the range.

Companion website

Go to the companion website at **www.pearsoned.co.uk/econexpress** to find more revision support online for this topic area.

Notes

And finally, before the assessment . . .

You should by now have developed your skills and knowledge in ways that can help you perform to the best of your ability, whatever the form of assessment used on your course.

At this stage you should be aware that your assessment may involve one of the following.

- **Assignment** where one or more extended problems must be answered in your own time with a specific deadline.
- **Examination** where a timed test is set in a specified location with a range of possible questions, such as:
  - *Multiple choice questions*
  - *Problem solving questions.*

Whatever the form of your assessment, the examiners will be looking to award marks for particular skills that you have displayed in your answers.

- **Accuracy** The ability to follow a set method and obtain the correct solution. For example, you may be able to find the prices required for a firm to maximise profit. You need to apply a standard mathematical procedure correctly and to demonstrate that you can produce successive lines of manipulation without making any numerical or algebraic mistakes.
- **Application** The ability to select the appropriate mathematical or statistical technique to solve a particular problem in economics. For example, you may be able to test the hypothesis that salaries in a firm are above the national average for that industry. To do this you need to suggest ways of collecting sample data and to choose the appropriate hypothesis test to analyse the data. The conclusions must be put in context.
- **Knowledge** The ability to recall basic mathematical and statistical facts and formulae. For example, you may be able quote the formula for the confidence limits for the difference of two means and the conditions under which the formula is valid.

How to approach and present assignments

Assignments will challenge you to write for different types of task, but the following steps will help you plan, structure and deliver your assignment whatever the task.

- **Realistic time planning:** Check the assignment submission date, work out how long you have from now to that date and allocate a specific amount of time each week to work on your assignment

- **Identify what you need to do:** Make sure you are clear on the type of task and have a thorough grasp of that topic. Have you been given a list of standard problems which can be solved using techniques taught in lectures or is it a more open-ended investigation requiring research or data collection?

- **Find and use relevant materials:** Read your notes and similar questions before you begin. If these are insufficient use the books recommended in the 'Read to Impress' section of this book. Use any other books or sources provided on the assignment brief. If you need to collect any statistical data think carefully about what this is going to be used for before you begin. Be realistic about the time you have to collect and analyse information obtained from the internet.

- **Structure your assignment:** Make sure that you:
  - Present work legibly and that you have written out your mathematical solutions clearly. Don't try to compress your answers. Write out any algebraic manipulation on separate lines and don't forget to explain your logic in words. It should be possible to read your mathematics out loud and make it sound like English prose.

  - Separate your assignment into identifiable sections even if this is just a list of questions and parts of questions. For a more open-ended assignment these should include an introduction, the main body of your answer and conclusions. Be selective when presenting statistical diagrams and results. Put some of these in appendices if necessary. Don't forget to interpret your answers in context.

  - Use a consistent referencing system, e.g. Harvard style. Reference from the text wherever appropriate (e.g., Sloman, J. 2013) and make sure that all technical data sources are identified clearly so that they can be checked.

- **Redraft your material:** Give yourself time in your plan for redrafting your first attempt. Check your work both for technical accuracy and clarity. Be prepared to produce second or third drafts which will invariably be better than the first!

How to approach your examination

- **Plan your revision:** Use a calendar to put dates in your planner and write in the dates of your exams. Fill in your targets each day. Be realistic when setting targets, and try your best to stick to them. If you miss a revision period, remember to re-schedule it for another time.
- **Check what will be examined and in what ways:** Identify the topics on your syllabus. Get to know the format of the papers – time, number of questions, types of questions.
- **Make a summary** of the key definitions, formulae and standard techniques relevant to each topic that you are revising.
- **Read again** the chapters of this book for each topic that you are revising. Make sure that you have worked through all the questions and can tick the 'confident' box for each element of the revision checklist at the end of each chapter.
- **Work out how long to spend on each section:** If your exam has different sections (multiple choice, short questions, long questions) allocate the appropriate time for each section before you begin. Use the number of marks available for each question to plan this.
- **Attempt as many past paper questions** as you can. Do the questions yourself before checking your answers. The online resources to this book contain many exam questions with fully worked solutions.

How to tackle your examination

What you do in the exam room depends, in part, on the type of question you are answering and whether you are given a choice of question.

Multiple choice questions

- Work out the number of minutes per question; e.g., 8 multiple choice questions in a 20 minute section is 2.5 minutes a question.
- Check that there is no penalty for wrong answers. If there is no penalty, make sure you attempt all questions.
- Don't spend too much time on any one question – leave it out and return later. Subsequent questions may be easier.
- It may be possible to use common-sense to rule out some of the answers and check others by substituting the values into the relevant equation instead of formally solving the problem.
- Towards the end of the exam, if you still have some remaining questions unanswered, have an intelligent guess rather than miss them out.

Problem solving questions

- If you have a choice of question, read each one carefully before deciding which question to answer.
- Answer your 'best question' first, to help gain confidence.
- Manage your time effectively. Try not to go over the time allocation for each question. If you have not finished in that time and are not about to finish, leave the question and move on. You can always come back to it later.
- Make sure that you answer the question set. It is all too easy to misread an algebraic term in a mathematical expression or a number in statistical data. Such a mistake can be costly in terms of marks and time.
- Read the whole question before you begin. It is tempting to answer the first part of a question before reading subsequent parts. However, as so often in mathematics, the parts may be interlinked, and knowing what is coming up may well influence how you tackle the first part.
- Make sure that you choose the appropriate statistical test before you perform the calculations. Check out the assumptions required for the validity of the test.
- Put your answers in context and check that they make sense in economic terms. The question may well be a particular case of a more general economic result which you know.
- Write out your mathematics neatly, putting each step on a separate line. Space your work out. Not only will this make it easy for the examiner to award you marks, but it will give you a better chance of spotting and correcting your mistakes.

 Final revision checklist

- ☐ Have you revised everything in the 'Revision Checklist' at the start of each chapter and topic?
- ☐ Have you used the books in the 'Read to Impress' section to make additional notes on any topic that you find difficult?
- ☐ Can you see how to do each 'Assessment question' after working through the 'Answer guidelines' at the end of each chapter?
- ☐ Have you checked your answers to the 'Test Yourself' questions with those provided on the companion website?
- ☐ Have you tried the extra multiple choice and specimen examination questions provided on the companion website?

Notes

And finally, before the assessment . . .

Notes

Glossary

Key mathematical terms

Average cost function Total cost per unit of output: $AC = TC/Q$.

Chain rule Differentiate the outer function and multiply by the derivative of the inner function:

$$\frac{dy}{dx} = \frac{dy}{du} \times \frac{du}{dx}.$$

Consumer's surplus Excess cost that the consumer would have been prepared to pay for goods over and above what was actually paid. If (Q_0, P_0) lies on a demand curve, $P = f(Q)$, then $CS = \int_0^{Q_0} f(Q)dQ - Q_0 P_0$.

Cross-price elasticity of demand The percentage change in demand divided by the percentage change in the price of an alternative good:

$$\frac{P_A}{Q} \times \frac{\partial Q}{\partial P_A}.$$

Discounting The process of working backwards in time to find the present values from a future value. The rate of interest is the discount rate.

Equilibrium (market) This state occurs when supply and demand are equal.

Exponential form A representation of a number expressed in powers such as b^n, where b is the base and n is the exponent.

Geometric progression A sequence of numbers in which you multiply by a fixed number to go from one term to the next. The multiplier is the geometric ratio and the sum of consecutive terms is a geometric series.

Homogeneous production function A function with the property that, when all of the inputs are multiplied by λ the output is multiplied by λ^n, where n is the degree of homogeneity. The function displays decreasing, constant or increasing returns to scale when $n < 1$, $n = 1$ or $n > 1$, respectively.

Identity matrix An $n \times n$ matrix, I, in which every entry on the main diagonal is the number one and all other entries are zero. If A is any $n \times n$ matrix then $AI = I = IA$.

Glossary

Income elasticity of demand Percentage change in demand divided by percentage change in income:

$$\frac{Y}{Q} \times \frac{\partial Q}{\partial Y}.$$

Inverse matrix If **A** and **B** are $n \times n$ matrices with the property that $\mathbf{AB} = \mathbf{I} = \mathbf{BA}$, then **A** and **B** are inverses of each other and we write $\mathbf{B} = \mathbf{A}^{-1}$.

Logarithm The power to which a base must be raised to yield a particular number: if $M = b^n$ then n is the logarithm of M to base b and we write $n = \log_b M$.

Marginal cost The cost of producing one more unit of output:

$$MC = \frac{d(TC)}{dQ}.$$

Marginal product of capital The change in output produced by one more unit of capital with labour held fixed:

$$MP_K = \frac{\partial Q}{\partial K}.$$

Marginal product of labour The change in output produced by one more unit of labour with capital held fixed:

$$MP_L = \frac{\partial Q}{\partial L}.$$

Marginal propensity to consume The increase in consumption when national income rises by one unit:

$$MPC = \frac{dC}{dY}.$$

Marginal propensity to save The increase in savings when national income rises by one unit:

$$MPS = \frac{dS}{dY} = 1 - MPC.$$

Marginal rate of technical substitution The amount that capital needs to rise to maintain a constant level of output when labour decreases by one unit:

$$MRTS = \frac{MP_L}{MP_K}.$$

Marginal revenue The change in revenue when quantity increases by one unit:

$$MR = \frac{d(TR)}{dQ}.$$

Natural logarithms Logarithms to base e: if $M = e^x$ then $x = \ln M$.

Partial derivative with respect to x The derivative obtained when f is differentiated with respect to x, with y held constant:

$$\frac{\partial f}{\partial x} \text{ or } f_x.$$

Price elasticity of supply (or demand) The percentage change in quantity divided by the percentage change in price:

$$E = \frac{P}{Q} \times \frac{\partial Q}{\partial P}.$$

Producer's surplus Excess revenue that the producer has actually received over and above the revenue that it was prepared to accept for the supply of its goods. If (Q_0, P_0) lies on a supply curve $P = g(Q)$, then $PS = Q_0 P_0 - \int_0^{Q_0} g(Q)dQ.$

Product rule Multiply each function by the derivative of the other and add:

$$\frac{d(uv)}{dx} = u\frac{dv}{dx} + v\frac{du}{dx}.$$

Profit Total revenue minus total cost: $\pi = TR - TC.$

Quadratic An expression of the form $ax^2 + bx + c.$

Quotient rule Bottom times derivative of top, minus top times derivative of bottom, all over bottom squared:

$$\frac{d}{dx}\left(\frac{u}{v}\right) = \frac{v\frac{du}{dx} - u\frac{dv}{dx}}{v^2}.$$

Stationary point A point on a curve where the gradient is zero. If the second-order derivative is positive (negative) the point is a minimum (maximum).

Total cost The sum of the fixed and variable costs: $TC = FC + (VC)Q.$

Total revenue A firm's total earnings from the sale of a good: $TR = PQ.$

Vector A matrix with either one row or one column.

Key statistical terms

Alternative hypothesis A statement, H_1, that the statistic being tested has increased, decreased or just changed from the value given in the null hypothesis.

Chi-squared test statistic A measure of how well a model fits a data set:

$$X^2 = \sum \frac{(O - E)^2}{E}.$$

Confidence interval An interval derived from a sample in which there is a specified probability that it contains the true population statistic. If the parent population is normal, and the variance of the parent population is known, the 95% confidence interval for a population mean is

$$\left(\bar{x} - 1.96\frac{\sigma}{\sqrt{n}}, \bar{x} + 1.96\frac{\sigma}{\sqrt{n}}\right).$$

Critical (or rejection) region The range of values of the test statistic that leads to the rejection of the null hypothesis.

Degrees of freedom Number of cells minus the number of restrictions. For a contingency table with m rows and n columns, this is $(m - 1) \times (n - 1)$.

Discrete random variable A variable, X, that takes specific values, x_i, with probability, p_i.

Expected frequencies in a contingency table Frequencies produced on the assumption that there is no association between the variables:

$$\frac{\text{row total times column total}}{\text{grand total}}.$$

Expected value of a discrete random variable Value found by summing the products, $x_i \, p_i$, in a probability distribution table: $E(X) = \sum x_i \, p_i$.

Independent events Events A and B where the occurrence of one does not affect the occurrence of the other: $P(A \text{ and } B) = P(A) \times P(B)$ (the multiplication law).

Interquartile range The difference between the upper and lower quartiles.

Line of best fit Minimises the sum of the squares of the residuals: $y = a + bx$ where

$$b = \frac{S_{xy}}{S_{xx}}$$

and $a = \bar{y} - b\bar{x}$.

Mean Sum of the values of a data set divided by the number of values:

$$\frac{1}{n}\sum_{i=1}^{n} x_i.$$

Median The middle value when data is arranged in order:

$$\text{median} = \frac{1}{2}(n + 1)\text{th item.}$$

Mode The most frequent item in a data set.

Mutually exclusive events Events A and B that cannot occur at the same time: $P(A \text{ or } B) = P(A) + P(B)$ (the addition law of probability).

Null hypothesis A statement, H_0, that a population statistic takes a particular value.

Order of a matrix A matrix with m rows and n columns has order $m \times n$.

Pearson's product moment correlation coefficient Measures the extent to which the points on a scatter diagram lie close to a straight line:

$$r = \frac{S_{xy}}{\sqrt{S_{xx}S_{yy}}}$$

where

$$S_{xy} = \sum x_i y_i - \frac{\sum x_i \sum y_i}{n}, \; S_{xx} = \sum x_i^2 - \frac{\left(\sum x_i\right)^2}{n}, \; S_{yy} = \sum y_i^2 - \frac{\left(\sum y_i\right)^2}{n}.$$

Probability of an event The number of outcomes in which the event occurs, divided by the total number of equally likely outcomes.

Quartiles The lower and upper quartiles are located one-quarter and three-quarters of the way along an ordered data set:

$$Q_1 = \frac{1}{4}(n + 1)\text{th item and}$$

$$Q_3 = \frac{3}{4}(n + 1)\text{th item.}$$

Random sampling Method of choosing a sample in which every possible sample has an equal chance of being picked.

Range The difference between the largest and smallest numbers in a data set.

Significance level The probability that the test statistic is in the critical region.

Spearman's rank correlation coefficient Measures the amount of agreement in the ranks of a data set:

$$\rho = 1 - \frac{6\sum d_i^2}{n(n^2 - 1)}.$$

Test statistic A number that you calculate from the sample in order to test out the null hypothesis.

Type I error Occurs when the null hypothesis, H_0, is rejected when it is true.

Type II error Occurs when the null hypothesis, H_0, is accepted when it is false (that is, when H_1 is true).

Variance Measures the spread of data about the mean:

$$\frac{1}{n}\sum(x - \bar{x})^2 = \frac{1}{n}\sum x^2 - \bar{x}^2.$$

This number is multiplied by $n/(n - 1)$ when estimating the population variance from the variance of a sample.

Notes

Read to impress

Here are some books that you can use to develop your answers on the topic area.

Barrow, M. (2012) *Statistics for Economics, Accounting and Business Studies*, 6th edition. Harlow, UK: Pearson Education.

Bradley, T. (2013) *Essential Mathematics for Economics and Business*, 4th edition. Chichester, UK: John Wiley & Sons.

Dowling, E. (2011) *Introduction to Mathematical Economics*, 3rd edition. New York: McGraw-Hill.

Jacques, I. (2012) *Mathematics for Economics and Business*, 7th edition. Harlow, UK: Pearson Education.

Renshaw, G. (2011) *Mathematics for Economics*, 3rd edition. Oxford: Oxford University Press.

Swift, L. and Piff, S. (2010) *Quantitative Methods: for Business, Management and Finance*, 3rd edition. Basingstoke, UK: Palgrave Macmillan.

Sydsaeter, K., Hammond, P. and Strom, A. (2012) *Essential Mathematics for Economic Analysis*, 4th edition. Harlow, UK: Pearson Education.

Waters, D. (2011) *Quantitative Methods for Business*, 5th edition. Harlow, UK: Pearson Education.

Wisniewski, M. (2013) *Mathematics for Economics: an Integrated Approach*, 3rd edition. Basingstoke, UK: Palgrave Macmillan.

- Read to impress

Notes

Index